THE SCIENCES

THE SCIENCES

A READING BOOK FOR CHILDREN

ASTRONOMY · PHYSICS · HEAT · LIGHT · SOUND
ELECTRICITY · MAGNETISM · CHEMISTRY
PHYSIOGRAPHY · METEOROLOGY

BY

EDWARD S. HOLDEN

YESTERDAY'S CLASSICS
CHAPEL HILL, NORTH CAROLINA

Cover and arrangement © 2009 Yesterday's Classics, LLC.

This edition, first published in 2009 by Yesterday's Classics, an imprint of Yesterday's Classics, LLC, is an unabridged republication of the text originally published by Ginn and Company in 1927. For the complete listing of the books that are published by Yesterday's Classics, please visit www.yesterdaysclassics.com. Yesterday's Classics is the publishing arm of the Baldwin Online Children's Literature Project which presents the complete text of hundreds of classic books for children at www.mainlesson.com.

ISBN-10: 1-59915-338-6

ISBN-13: 978-1-59915-338-4

Yesterday's Classics, LLC
PO Box 3418
Chapel Hill, NC 27515

TO
MY YOUNG FRIEND
Mildred Greble

PREFACE

THE object of the present volume is to present chapters to be read in school or at home that shall materially widen the outlook of American school children in the domain of science, and of the applications of science to the arts and to daily life. It is in no sense a text-book, although the fundamental principles underlying the sciences treated are here laid down. Its main object is to help the child to understand the material world about him.

All natural phenomena are orderly; they are governed by law; they are not magical. They are comprehended by some one; why not by the child himself? It is not possible to explain every detail of a locomotive to a young pupil, but it is perfectly practicable to explain its principles so that this machine, like others, becomes a mere special case of certain well-understood general laws.

The general plan of the book is to waken the imagination; to convey useful knowledge; to open the doors towards wisdom. Its special aim is to stimulate observation and to excite a living and lasting interest in the world that lies about us. The sciences of astronomy, physics, chemistry, meteorology, and physiography are treated as fully and as deeply as the conditions permit; and the lessons that they teach are enforced by examples taken from familiar and important things. In astronomy, for example, emphasis is laid upon phenomena that the child himself can observe, and he is instructed how to go about it. The rising and setting of the stars, the phases of the moon, the uses of the telescope, are explained in simple words. The mystery of these and other matters is not magical, as the child first supposes. It is to deeper mysteries that his attention is here directed. Mere phenomena are treated as special cases of very general laws. The same process is followed in the exposition of the other sciences.

Familiar phenomena, like those of steam, of shadow, of reflected light, or musical instruments, of echoes, etc., are referred to their fundamental causes. Whenever it is desirable, simple experiments are described and fully illustrated, and all such experiments can very well be repeated in the schoolroom.

Finally, the book has been thrown into the form of a conversation between children. It is hoped that this has been accomplished without the pedantry of *Sandford and Merton* (although it must be frankly confessed that the principal interlocutor has his knowledge very well in hand for an undergraduate in vacation time) or the sentimentality of other modern books which need not be named here. The volume is the result of a sincere belief that much can be done to aid young children to comprehend the material world in which they live and of a desire to have a part in a work so very well worth doing.

EDWARD S. HOLDEN

CONTENTS

Introductory Chapter．．．．．．．．．．．．．．．．．．．．ー 1
Astronomy．．．．．．．．．．．．．．．．．．．．．．．．．．．．．．．ー 9
Physics．．．．．．．．．．．．．．．．．．．．．．．．．．．．．．．．．．．ー 77
Chemistry．．．．．．．．．．．．．．．．．．．．．．．．．．．．．．．ー 161
Meteorology．．．．．．．．．．．．．．．．．．．．．．．．．．．．．ー 175
Physiography．．．．．．．．．．．．．．．．．．．．．．．．．．．．ー 199

INTRODUCTORY CHAPTER

(To be read by the children who own this book)

LET me tell you how this book came to be written. Once upon a time, not so very long ago, a lot of children were spending the summer together in the country. Tom and Agnes were brother and sister and were together all the day long; bicycling or playing golf in the morning, reading or studying in the afternoon. The people who lived in the village used to call them the *inseparables* because they were always seen together during their whole vacation from June to September.

Their cousins Fred and Mary always spent a part of every summer with them; and when they came there were four inseparables, not two. The children liked the same games, liked to read the same books, to talk about the same kind of things, and so they got on very well together; though sometimes the two boys would go off by themselves for a hard day's tramp in the hills, or to shoot woodchucks, or for a very long bicycle ride, leaving their sisters at home to play in the garden with dolls, or to do fancywork and embroidery, or to play tennis, or to read a book together. Tom was thirteen years old then, and his sister Agnes was nine; cousin Fred was ten and his sister Mary was twelve.

THE SCIENCES

When the summer afternoons began to get very warm, in July, a rule was made that the children should spend them in the house, or on the wide, shady porch, or else under the trees on the lawn, or in the garden. Golf, tennis, and wheeling had to be done in the morning; the afternoons were to be spent in something different. Tom's father used to say that the proverb

All work and no play
Makes Jack a dull boy

was only half a proverb. It was just as true, he said, that

All play and no work
Makes Jack a sad shirk.

And so a part of every summer afternoon was given up to reading some good book, or to study, or to work of some sort. The two boys had their guns and wheels to keep thoroughly bright and clean, and a dozen other things of the sort; the two girls had sewing to do; and all of them together agreed to keep the pretty garden free from weeds.

Almost any afternoon you might see the four inseparables tucked away in a corner of the broad piazza, each one busy about something, and all talking and laughing—except, of course, when one of them was reading, and the others paying good attention. Tom's big brother Jack was at home from college, and in the afternoons he was almost always on the porch reading, or else on the green lawn lying under the trees; and Tom's older sisters, Mabel and Eleanor, were there too, sewing, or embroidering, or reading, or talking together.

INTRODUCTORY CHAPTER

FIGURE 1   THE PORCH

So there were two groups, the four children—the inseparables—and the three older ones. When the children came to something in their book that they did not quite understand, Tom would call out to his big brother Jack to explain it to them, and Jack would usually get up and come over to where the children were and tell them what they wanted to know. Almost every day there were conversations of the sort, and explanations by some one of the older ones to the four children. All kinds of questions would come up, like these:

"Jack, tell us why a 'possum pretends to be dead when he is only frightened and wants to get away."

"Jack, tell us why a rifle shoots so much straighter than a shot-gun or a musket."

"Jack, what's the reason that a lobster hasn't red blood?" or else:

THE SCIENCES

"Eleanor, what is the difference between a fern and a tree?"

"Is that coral bead made by an animal or an insect?"

"What is amber, anyway?" and so on.

The children had no end of questions to ask, and Jack or one of the older girls could generally answer them. When they could not give a complete answer the dictionary was brought out; and if that was not enough, a volume of the encyclopædia. Sometimes the questions were talked over at the dinner table and the whole family had something to say. Tom's father had traveled a great deal and could almost always tell the children some real "true" story—something that had happened to himself personally, or that he had read.

The chapters in this book are conversations that the children had among themselves or with older people. They are written down here in fewer words than those actually spoken, but the meaning is the same.

When the children were talking about electric bells, for instance, they actually strung a wire from one end of the long porch to the other, and put a real bell at one end of it and a push button and a battery at the other. In this book there is a picture showing exactly what they did; but, after all, you cannot understand an electric bell half so well by a picture as you can by the real bell and the real wire.[1] So when one of the children who is reading

---

[1] Children should be careful to read the titles printed under each picture with attention. The titles explain what the picture means.

INTRODUCTORY CHAPTER

FIGURE 2 A CELL OF DRY BATTERY

The two wires are to be fastened to the two screw posts in the picture—one at the left-hand side, and one in the middle, of the top of the cell.

this book comes to an experiment he must read all that the book says about it, and understand it as well as he can. If he can get an electric battery, and a bell, and wire, and a push button, then the picture in this book will tell him exactly how to join them together; and when he has done this and actually tried the experiment—and made it succeed—he will know as much about electric bells as he needs to know.

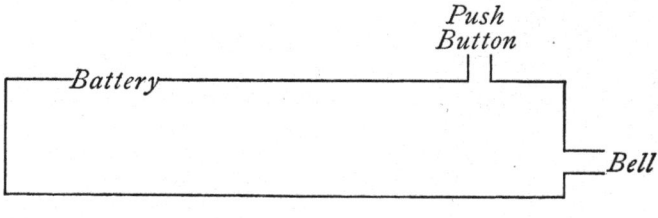

FIGURE 3

If he cannot get the bell and the wire, and so forth, he can probably see a bell of the sort somewhere; and if he keeps his eyes open and thinks about what he has read, he can certainly understand how it works. Here is the battery always trying to send out a stream of electricity along any wires joined to the two screws at the top. Here is the wire, which is almost a complete loop—almost but not quite. If the loop were continuous,—if the wire were all in one piece,—then the stream of electricity would flow along the wire from the battery and would ring the bell.

The use of the push button is to make the wire continuous—to join the two ends of it so that the stream of electricity can pass along it. When you have done this—when you have joined the ends of the loop of wire—the bell rings, and only then, which is just as it should be.

This book gives the pictures and the explanations. They can be understood by paying attention; and when they are once understood a great number of things will be clear that all children ought to know, and that have to be learned sometime. Why not now? The sooner the better.

FIGURE 4 AN ELECTRIC BELL

The wires are fastened to the two screws at the bottom of the box.

If you read what is written in the book and perfectly understand it, that is very well. If there is an experiment to be tried, and you can get the things to try it with, so much the better. If you have any trouble in understanding, ask some one—your father, your mother, your teacher—to explain to you. If you can find another book—a dictionary or an

INTRODUCTORY CHAPTER

encyclopædia—that describes the same experiment, read that too. Perhaps it will tell you what you want to know, better, or more simply, or more fully, or in a different way. Then, finally, keep your eyes open to actually see in the world the things that are talked about in this book. When you see them try to understand them. Remember what you have read here, and you will find that you understand a good many things that you see about you every day. Somebody understands these things,—push buttons, electric lamps, telescopes, and so forth. Why should not you? You can if you pay attention enough. The world is, after all, your world. It belongs to you as much as it belongs to any one. The things in it can all be explained and understood. It is everybody's business to *try* to understand them at any rate. All these things concern you. The more you know about them, the better citizen you can be—the more useful to your country, to your friends, and to yourself.

FIGURE 5 A PUSH BUTTON

The two wires are fastened to two screws inside the push button.

THE MOON
The moon from a photograph taken with the great telescope of the Lick Observatory.

ASTRONOMY

THE SCIENCE OF THE SUN, MOON, AND STARS

The Earth as a Planet.—The children were looking at a map of the world one fine afternoon and studying the way the land and water are distributed, when Agnes said: "I never knew before how little land there was on the earth. Why, there is *very* much more water than land." "Oh, yes," said Tom, "there's very much more water on the surface; but it's all land at the bottom of the ocean. The sea is about three miles deep, you know, and then you come to the ocean bottom, and that is solid land again. The earth is nearly all rocks and soil; only a little of it is water, after all, but that little is on the surface, of course, and that is why it shows."

Agnes. So the earth is almost all land; if you dig down deep enough, you should come to rocks, even below the oceans?

Tom. Yes, and if you went up high enough, you would come to nothing. You would come to air first, and then by and by to no air, and then you would come to just nothing—to empty space.

Agnes. Well, it isn't quite empty, as you call it. There are other globes in space. There are other planets, and

FIGURE 6. AMERICA

FIGURE 7. THE OLD WORLD

the sun and the moon, and there are simply thousands of stars. So space isn't empty; it is pretty full!

Distance of the Moon and of the Sun from the Earth.—Here Tom's big brother Jack looked up from his book and said: "Well, that depends on what you call full. It is 240,000 miles from here to the moon, and the moon is the very nearest of all the heavenly bodies to us. There is a good deal of empty space between us and the moon, it seems to me."

Agnes. Two hundred and forty thousand miles! Oh, Jack, is that right?

Jack. Why, that isn't a beginning; how far off do you suppose the sun is? It is 93,000,000 miles—millions this time, not thousands; and some of the planets are much farther off yet, and every one of the stars is farther off still.

Agnes. Jack, tell us about it, will you? We don't know, and you do.

Jack. The very first thing you have to think about is the size of the earth. How far is it through and through the earth, Tom? If you pushed a stick through the earth from New York to China, how long would the stick be?

The Diameter of the Earth.—*Tom.* The geography says that the diameter of the earth is 8000 miles; so the stick would have to be 8000 miles long,—as long as from Cape Horn to Hudson Bay, my teacher says.

Jack. That's about right. Suppose there were a

THE SCIENCES

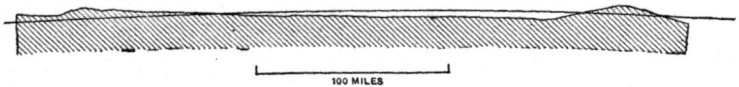

FIGURE 8

This picture shows the height of land on the earth compared to the depth of the sea. If you could cut the earth through and through with a knife and look at one part only, it would look something like the picture. All the shaded part is land. The curved line drawn all across the picture, near the top, is the curve of the surface of the oceans. Part of one of the oceans is shown by the white space below this curved line and above the floor of the ocean itself,—the shaded land. The curve of the ocean surface is continued across the picture underneath the mountains. If the surface of the earth were all water, the bounding line would be this curve. From side to side of the picture is about 350 miles. If the whole circle of the earth were drawn, it would be about eight feet in diameter. That is the scale of the drawing.

railway from Hudson Bay to Cape Horn, and express trains running on it at the rate of 40 miles an hour. Let us see how long they would take to go the 8000 miles. They would go 40 miles in one hour, and 80 miles in two hours, and 960 miles in a day—say 1000 miles a day. Well, they would take eight days to go the 8000 miles, then. Now, suppose we could build a railway to the moon. How long would an express train take to go the distance? Take your pencil, Tom, and cipher it out.

Tom. You said the distance from the earth to the moon was 240,000 miles. If the train goes 1000 miles a day, it would take 240 days. I don't need any pencil.

Jack. Sure enough; and 240 days is eight months (8 x 30 = 240). It would take the train eight months to go from the earth to the moon, then—eight whole months, traveling night and day at forty miles and more every hour.

Agnes. I should be nearly a year older when I got there than when I started, then.

Jack. Yes, and recollect that there are no stations on the railway to the moon. The moon is the heavenly

FIGURE 9   A BALLOON

Balloons carrying men have gone up more than five miles, and small balloons carrying thermometers, etc., have been sent nearly ten miles high. The atmosphere of the earth extends upwards a hundred miles or so, but beyond this there is no air—nothing but empty space.

THE SCIENCES

FIGURE 10 THE FULL MOON RISING IN THE EAST

body that is nearest to us, so that space is pretty nearly empty, after all.

Distance of the Sun from the Earth.—*Tom.* How far did you say it was from the earth to the sun—93,000,000 miles?

Jack. That's right. You will need your pencil to figure out how long the express train would take to go from the earth to the sun, Tom.

Tom. Yes, it is like this, isn't it? The train goes 1000 miles in a day; then it will take 93,000 days to get to get to the sun.

      30 x 93000   days
      12 x 3100   months
      258 1/2   years

ASTRONOMY

It would take 3100 months, that is more than 258 years, to get to the sun. That's a long journey! You would have 258 birthdays on the road, Agnes.

Jack. Put it this way, Tom: You all know that the Pilgrims landed at Plymouth Rock in 1620. Suppose that one of those Pilgrims, directly after he had landed from the ship, decided to take a train to the sun. He would have had to travel until the year 1878 (1620 + 258 = 1878); that is, if he had lived to make the journey. Even the wild elephant, which is thought to live at the most 150 years, would not survive a journey of 258 years.

Tom. Two hundred and fifty-eight years!

FIGURE 11 THE PILGRIMS LANDING ON PLYMOUTH ROCK FROM THEIR SHIP, THE "MAYFLOWER," DEC. 20, 1620

THE SCIENCES

The Planets Mercury and Venus.—*Jack*. Yes, and nearly all that space is empty too. There are only two planets between the earth and the sun—Mercury and Venus.

Agnes. Venus, the evening star?

Jack. Yes, Venus is the evening star sometimes. Venus and Mercury are the only planets that the Pilgrim would pass on the road from earth to the sun. Space is rather empty, isn't it?

Agnes. Aren't there any stars in between the earth and the sun, Jack?

Jack. Not one; the real stars are thousands and thousands of times farther off. We call Venus the "evening star," but Venus is not a star at all, but a planet. Let me tell you, so that you can make a sort of picture of it all in your minds. The sun is there in the middle of space and all the planets move around him, just as the earth does. Nearest to the sun is the planet Mercury, and then comes the planet Venus, and then the planet Earth.

Agnes. That sounds queerly— "the planet Earth"— though of course we know the Earth *is* a planet.

The Planets Mars, Jupiter, Saturn, Uranus,[1] and Neptune.—*Jack*. Yes, exactly so. And then there are other planets farther away from the sun than the earth; Mars for one, and then Jupiter, and then Saturn, and then Uranus, and then Neptune. That is all we know

---

[1] Pronounced ū′ra-nus.

of; there may be more of them. Neptune is thirty times as far from the sun as the earth is. Here is a little table that I will write down for you to keep. You need not memorize it, only recollect that Mercury and Venus are nearer to the sun than we are, and that all the others are farther away.

Distances of the Planets from the Sun

The planet *Mercury* is 36 million miles from the sun
The planet *Venus* is 67 million miles from the sun
The planet *Earth* is 93 million miles from the sun
The planet *Mars* is 141 million miles from the sun
The planet *Jupiter* is 483 million miles from the sun
The planet *Saturn* is 886 million miles from the sun
The planet *Uranus* is 1782 million miles from the sun
The planet *Neptune* is 2791 million miles from the sun

Jupiter is five times, and Neptune is thirty times, as far from the sun as the earth is.

Tom. Isn't there a map of all these planets that we can see?

Jack. No, and there's a good reason why. Suppose you tried to make a map of them, and suppose you took the distance from the sun to the Earth on the map to be an inch. Don't you see that the distance from the Sun to Neptune would have to be thirty times one inch, and the page of your book thirty inches wide—nearly a yard wide?

Tom. Of course, no book has a page as big as that; but you might make little maps.

How to Make a Map that Shows the Sun and Planets.— *Jack.* You and Agnes can make a map yourselves tomorrow morning, if you want to, when you go out for a walk, and I'll tell you how to do it.

FIGURE 12 A SCHOOL GLOBE

Suppose you take the large globe in the library, that you were looking at just now, to stand for the Sun. It is two feet in diameter. Well, the diameter of the real sun is 870,000 miles, and your map has to be made all to one scale. Every step of yours is about two feet long, isn't it, Tom? Try it.

Tom. Yes, my steps are almost exactly two feet long.

Jack. Well, remember to-morrow that every step you take along the road to the village is really two feet long, but that it stands on the map for 870,000 miles.

Agnes. Are we going to make the map along the road?

Jack. My dear, you have to do it that way; your map is going to be nearly a mile and a quarter long. You have to use the whole country round to make it.

Agnes. Well, that *is* a map!

Tom. How shall we make it, Jack?

Jack. You start, you know, with this globe in the house to stand for the Sun. The globe is two feet in diameter, and the real Sun is 870,000 miles in diameter.

ASTRONOMY

FIGURE 13　THE ROAD TO THE VILLAGE

Scale of the Map.—"So, recollect, every two feet on your map is 870,000 miles. Every one of your steps, Tom, stands for 870,000 miles.

"You must take with you
- a very small grain of canary-bird seed to stand for the planet *Mercury;*
- a very small green pea to stand for the planet *Venus;*
- a common green pea to stand for the planet *Earth;*
- a rather large pin out of Agnes' work box, and let its round head stand for the planet *Mars;*
- an orange to stand for the planet *Jupiter;*
- a golf ball to stand for the planet *Saturn;*
- a common marble to stand for the planet *Uranus;*
- a rather large marble to stand for the planet *Neptune.*

THE SCIENCES

FIGURE 14

The sizes of the planets of the solar system (the sun's family) compared with each other.

♄ = Saturn; ♃ = Jupiter; ♆ = Neptune; ♅ = Uranus; ♂ = Mars; ☾ = our Moon; ⊕ = Earth; ♀ = Venus; ☿ = Mercury.

Sizes of the Planets Compared to the Sun.—"If this globe, two feet in diameter, stands for the Sun (which is really 870,000 miles in diameter), then a common green pea is just the right size to stand for the Earth (which is really 8000 miles in diameter) and an orange is just the right size to stand for Jupiter, and so on. You are going to carry all the planets off in your pocket, and when you have put them down in the right places you have made your map."

Tom. How shall we know where to put them down?

Jack. I will give you the right number of steps to take between the Sun and every one of the planets. If one of Tom's steps is 870,000 miles, then:

Mercury (the canary seed) is
   41 steps from the Sun (the globe at the house)
Venus (the small pea) is
   77 steps from the globe that stands for the Sun
Earth (the pea) is
   107 steps from the globe that stands for the Sun
Mars (the pin's head) is
   162 steps from the globe that stands for the Sun
Jupiter (the orange) is
   555 steps from the globe that stands for the Sun
Saturn (the golf ball) is
   1019 steps from the globe that stands for the Sun
Uranus (the small marble) is
   2048 steps from the globe that stands for the Sun
Neptune (the large marble) is
   3208 steps from the globe that stands for the Sun.

Those are the right distances, and you can make your map tomorrow morning when you go for a walk. Recollect that the globe in the house stands for the Sun. You are to walk away from it along the road to the village until you've take 41 steps. Stop there and put down the canary seed to stand for the planet Mercury. Then go on 36 steps more and you will be 77 steps from the model of the Sun. This will be the place to put the small green pea that stands for the planet Venus; then go on 30 steps more and you will be 107 steps away from the Sun. This will be the place to put down the green pea that stands for the Earth, and so on. The last planet—Neptune—will be 3208 steps away from the house,—about one and a fifth miles away.

Agnes. I don't believe we can count such large

THE SCIENCES

numbers, Jack; we shall be sure to forget them and lose the count.

Jack. True enough, Agnes. Let me see if I can't make it simpler for you. I will write down on a card all that you have to remember, and we can make the numbers that you have to count smaller. We can do it this way; instead of counting the distances from the Sun to each planet, we will count the number of steps between each planet and the next one: this way. Here is the card that Jack wrote:

If one of Tom's steps is 870,000 miles, then:

The distance from the model of the Sun to the canary seed that stands for the planet Mercury is 41 steps; the distance from Mercury to Venus is 36 steps farther; the distance from Venus to the Earth is 30 steps farther; the distance from the Earth to Mars is 55 steps farther; the distance from Mars to Jupiter is 393 steps farther; the distance from Jupiter to Saturn is 464 steps farther; the distance from Saturn to Uranus is 1029 steps farther; the distance from Uranus to Neptune is 1160 steps farther.

NOTE.—The numbers that are needed to make the map are obtained in this way: If one step is 870,000 miles, then

Distance from the Sun to	Miles	Steps	Differences
Mercury	36,000,000	41	—
Venus	67,200,000	77	36

Earth	92,900,000	107	30
Mars	141,000,000	162	55
Jupiter	483,000,000	555	393
Saturn	886,000,000	1019	464
Uranus	1,782,000,000	2048	1029
Neptune	2,791,000,000	3208	1160

In the last column are the differences between the numbers just preceding: 77 less 41 is 36, 107 less 77 is 30, 162 less 107 is 55, and so on. If the model of the planet Mercury must be 41 steps from the model of the Sun, and if the model of the planet Venus must be 77 steps from the Sun, then the model of Venus must be 30 steps away from the model of Mercury, and so on for the others.

When the next day came, Tom and Agnes set out to make the map of the Sun and all the planets. The school globe in the house stood for the Sun, and they carried the models of the planets with them, as well as the card that showed how far apart the planets were to be on the scale of their map. Agnes kept the card in her hand and told Tom how many steps he was to take. At the house she said: "Tom, you must take 41 steps, and then stop." So Tom walked off, counting his steps till he had made 41, then he put down the little canary seed that stood for the planet Mercury. The globe in the library stood for the Sun; this tiny seed stood for the planet Mercury; the distance from the globe to the seed stood for the real distance of the real planet Mercury from the real Sun. Thirty-six steps farther they put down the small green pea that stood for the planet Venus; and 30 steps farther still they put down the green pea that was to stand for the Earth.

Here they stopped for a minute to think about it all. This little bit of a green pea was the huge Earth, very, very much smaller than the globe that stood for the Sun. They could not even see the small green pea that stood for Venus, nor the little seed that stood for Mercury, though they knew about where they were, of course. There were no other planets in the real space between the real Earth and the real Sun except just those two, Mercury and Venus, and space *was* almost empty, after all, as Jack had said, except for few, very few, planets that were exceedingly far apart. "Why, we

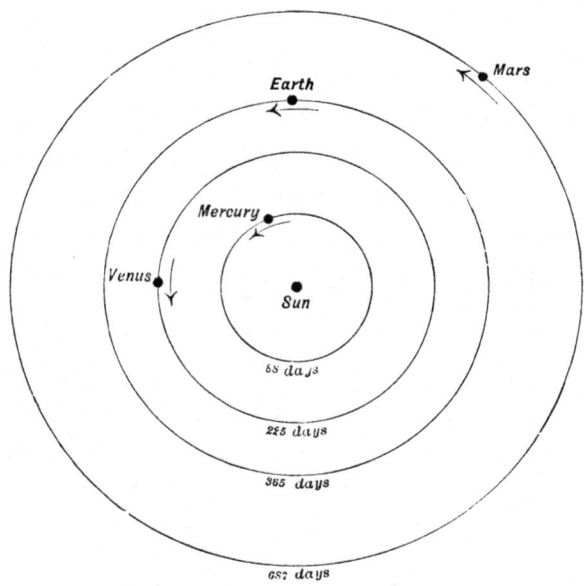

FIGURE 15
A plan of the orbits of Mercury, Venus, the Earth, and Mars.

can't even see the models of Mercury and Venus from here," said Agnes. "No," said Tom, "but if they were shining things, as the planets are, we could see them. They ought to be painted white so that the sunlight would make them glisten."

So the children went on putting the models down in the road at the right distances apart. Agnes read the right numbers from the card, and Tom walked away counting his steps up to the thousands. He got rather tired of it, but they kept on until finally all the models were put down at the right distances apart, and their map was made. By this time they were nearly a mile and a quarter away from home, and they had spent the whole morning in the work. But the work was not wasted. They really understood what they had been doing, and realized, as very few people—even grown people—do, how immensely large space is, and how few—very few—planets there are to fill it.[1]

When the children came home that day there was a great deal of talk about the map—the model—that they had made. All the older people and some of the neighbors were interested in it. They found their work had not been wasted and that they had really learned something.

---

[1] It is strongly recommended that the teacher should make such a model of the solar system as has just been described, with the aid of his pupils. If actually made, it will lead to a true and living realization of the dimensions of the solar system. No amount of mere class-room instruction can do this for young children.

THE SCIENCES

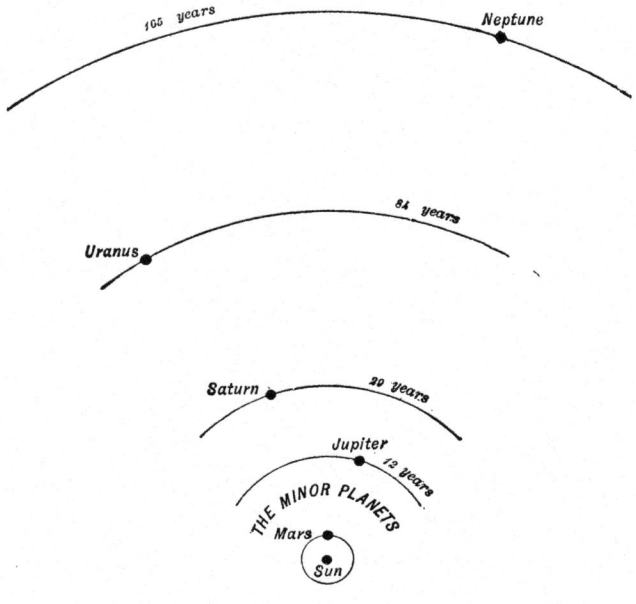

FIGURE 16
A plan of the orbits of Mars, Jupiter, Saturn, Uranus, and Neptune. (The scale of this drawing is much smaller than that of the preceding one.)

The Solar System; the Sun and Planets.—Jack told them some interesting things about the sun and the planets. They knew already, of course, that all the planets moved round the sun in paths that were called *orbits*. The earth, for instance, goes once round the sun every year,—every 365 ¼ days. Every one of the planets goes round the sun, too, in its own particular orbit, in its own year. For instance,

> Mercury goes round the Sun in 88 days = about 3 months
> Venus goes round the Sun in 225 days = about 7 months
> Earth goes round the Sun in 365 days = about 12 months

ASTRONOMY

> Mars goes round the Sun in 687 days = about 23 months
> Jupiter goes round the Sun in 12 years
> Saturn goes round the Sun in 29 years
> Uranus goes round the Sun in 84 years
> Neptune goes round the Sun in 165 years

Tom's father told them about one of the kings of Spain who, long ago, used to play chess on a huge chessboard with real living persons for chessmen. These men moved from square to square on the chessboard as the game went on; and Tom's father said that the map of the solar system with its eight planets ought to have had eight little boys who would walk in circles round the model of the sun, carrying the models of the planets in their hands. One boy would carry the canary seed that stood for Mercury, and he would have to walk once round his circle in three months; another boy would carry the small green pea that stood for Venus, and he would have to walk around a larger circle once in seven months; still another would carry the green pea that stood for the Earth, and he would have to walk around the circle of the Earth's orbit once in each year; and so on for all the other planets. The boy that carried the marble that stood for Neptune would not get all the way around his circle for 165 years. "He would be quite grown up by the time he got round, wouldn't he?" said Agnes. "Well," said Jack, "Papa is right; that is the real way to make the model. The sun is in the middle. All the planets move round him in circles; each one of the planets takes a different time to go once around its orbit. All of these planets together make up the solar system,—the family of the sun."

THE SCIENCES

Tom. Why do they call it the *solar* system, Jack?

Jack. Just because it is the sun's system; *sol*, in Latin, means "the sun," and solar means "belonging to the sun." All the planets go round the sun, and round nothing else. That's why. The sun is so much larger than any of the planets, or than all of them put together for that matter, that it is the sun's system.

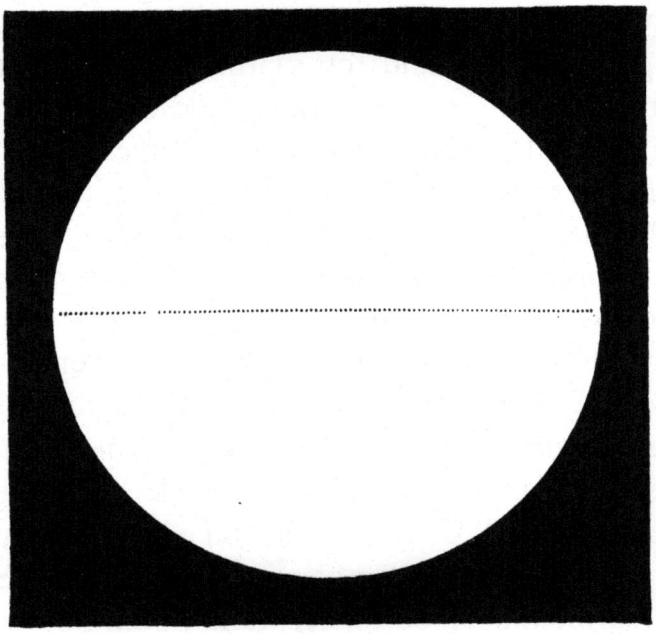

Figure 17

In this picture the large circle stands for the sun. Each of the small dots stands for the earth. The size of the dots and of the circle are in the right proportion. It would take 109 earths in a row stretched across the disk of the sun to reach from edge to edge. Count them.

ASTRONOMY

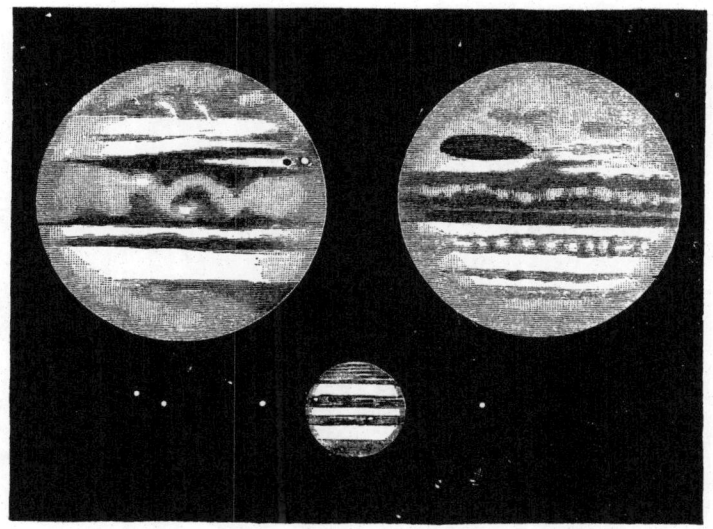

Figure 18

Three drawings of Jupiter as seen in a telescope. The lower drawing shows Jupiter with his four bright satellites. It is on a smaller scale than the others.

Relative Sizes of the Planets.—"You see," said Jack, "that the sun is very large indeed. He is as much larger than the earth as the library globe is larger than a green pea. If all the solar system were to shrink and shrink until the earth—the huge earth—had shrunk to the size of one green pea, the sun would still be as big as the globe in the library—it would be two feet in diameter."

The real diameters of the sun and planets are:

The Sun   is   866,400 miles in diameter

The smaller planets

Mercury   is   3,030 miles in diameter

Venus   is   7,700 miles in diameter

FIGURE 19

Drawings of the planet Saturn as seen in a telescope at different times. In the upper figure we are looking at Saturn's rings edgewise, and they appear as a thin line. In the next drawing we are looking down on the rings. In the third drawing we are also looking down on the rings.

The Earth	is	7,918 miles in diameter
The Moon	is	2,162 miles in diameter
Mars	is	4,230 miles in diameter

The giant planets

Jupiter	is	86,500 miles in diameter
Saturn	is	73,000 miles in diameter
Uranus	is	31,900 miles in diameter
Neptune	is	34,800 miles in diameter

"Oh!" said Agnes, "we left the Moon out of our model."

"So we did," said Tom; "let us go this afternoon and stick a pin in the ground to stand for the Moon, alongside of the green pea that stands for the Earth."

The Moons of the Planets.—"Well," said Jack, "that's all right. Only you must choose a pin with a very small head. And, while you are about it, you had better put in some more pins, for several of the other planets have moons—*satellites*, they are called—and they go around their planets just as the Moon goes around the Earth. Mercury has no satellite that we know of; Venus has no satellite that we know of; the Earth has the Moon for satellite; Mars has two very small satellites; Jupiter has four large satellites about the size of our Moon, and five extremely small ones; Saturn has nine satellites, one larger than our Moon; Uranus has four satellites;

FIGURE 20   THE STARLIT SKY

Neptune has one satellite almost the same size as our Moon."

The Minor Planets; the Asteroids.—"Yes, and at the same time you might as well sprinkle about 500 grains of sand in the space between Mars and Jupiter to stand for the 500 minor planets that they call *asteroids*. There are about 500 of them known now, and, I've no doubt, hundreds more not yet discovered. When you read in the newspaper that a new planet was discovered last night by some astronomer, that means that another one of these minor planets has been found. They find them by photography with a large telescope."

FIGURE 21   THE GREAT COMET OF 1858

THE SCIENCES

Comets.—"And, by the way, put in two or three thin wisps of cotton wool somewhere to stand for comets. Comets are mostly made out of shining gas—they aren't solid. But they look a little like wisps of cotton wool, anyway."

Tom. Is that all? Shall we put in anything else?

Jack. That is all for the solar system, except clouds of very little stones, almost like dust, that make the *shooting stars* or *meteors*.

The Stars.—"What about the stars?" said Agnes.

Jack. Oh, the stars are not part of the solar system, Agnes; they are millions and millions of miles outside of it; the very nearest star is thousands and thousands of times farther from us than even the planet Neptune.

Tom. How far off are they, Jack, anyway? Could we get the nearest of the stars on our model? Where would it be? In the next country?

Distances of the Stars.—"Let me see," said Jack, "the nearest star of all is 20,000,000,000,000 miles from the sun— twenty millions of millions of miles! If you were to put it on your map, it would have to be about 9000 miles from where we are now—it would have to be somewhere in China."

Agnes. Is that the *nearest* star, Jack?

Jack. Yes, the very nearest. If you should put another school globe in the Chinese emperor's palace at Peking, that would stand for the nearest star to our sun, which our school globe in the library stands for. The sun is a star, and stars are about of the same size. So a school globe may stand for any one of them.

Tom. Well, space *is* empty if planets and stars aren't any closer than that. What is the difference between a planet and a star, anyway?

What is a Planet?—"The greatest difference," said Jack, "is this: the stars shine by their own light, just as an electric street lamp shines; and the planets shine by light reflected from the sun, just as a football would shine if you held it up in the sunlight."

Tom. Do you mean that Venus and Jupiter do not shine by their own light?

Jack. I mean just that. Venus and Jupiter are two great globes something like the earth, made out of rocks and soil, with clouds all around them—clouds something like our clouds. The sun shines on them, and they shine, and we see them. If the sun were to stop shining on them, they'd go out like a candle.

Agnes. But, Jack, Venus shines at night, in the dark sky, when the sun *has* stopped shining.

Jack. The sun has stopped shining on you and me at night because the earth has turned round and we are in the earth's shadow; you know that. But all the while the sun is shining just the same. It is shining on the other side of the earth, where it is daytime, and it is sending out sunbeams above the earth and below it, everywhere all the time. Some of these sunbeams fall on Jupiter and Venus and make them bright, and we see them. What we really see is the sun's brightness reflected back to us, just as you might see an electric light at night shining on a mirror. You might be in the dark yourself; the electric light might be round the corner of the street, but the mirror would be bright.

Tom. So planets are bright because the sun shines on them. Why are the stars bright then?

Jack. Stars are bright just as the sun is bright. The sun makes its own light as an electric lamp makes *its* own light. The stars are like the sun. They shine by their own light. Planets shine by borrowed light. They borrow their light from the sun. If you were to go off and sit on the nearest star and look at the solar system, you might see the sun in the middle of it shining away all the time—all day and all night, too. And if you could see our little group of eight planets wheeling around it, they would be bright on the side nearest the sun—on the side shined upon; and be dark on the side away from the sun. The sunlight cannot go through them. The sun can shine only on that part of a planet that is turned towards it.

Phases of the Moon (New Moon, Full Moon, etc.).— "Don't you know the moon is often only half bright, and sometimes three-quarters bright, and so on? Venus looks that way in a telescope sometimes; in a telescope you can see Venus like a crescent moon—like a sickle. You do not see it like that with your eye, because Venus is so bright that your eyes are dazzled. You see the glare, and it looks like any other dazzling glare; you do not see its true shape."

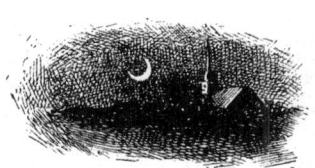

FIGURE 22
THE NEW MOON SETTING IN THE WEST

FIGURE 23
THE MOON IN THE FIRST QUARTER

FIGURE 24 FRED WATCHING THE FULL MOON RISE IN THE EAST

THE SCIENCES

Tom. You can't see the true shape of a sheet of tin that the sun shines on; it looks just like a dazzle of light.

Jack. That is the way with the planets when you do not use a telescope. Now the moon looks so large, and the light from any part of it is so faint, that you *can* see its shape. It does not dazzle your eyes. They call those different shapes of the bright part of the moon its *phases*. Venus has phases, too. The moon is a globe, you know, about 2000 miles in diameter. One half of it is always turned towards the sun, and that half of it is always bright, day and night. If we were on the sun, we should always see the whole circle of the moon bright.

FIGURE 25

A schoolroom experiment to show how the sun lights up half of every one of the planets, and only half. The room should be darkened; the lamp should have a ground-glass shade; the orange that stands for the earth or planet should be fastened by a knitting needle to a pincushion. The pupils should see that half, and only half, of a globe (a planet, the earth, the moon) is illuminated. They should also see that by going to different parts of the room different portions (phases) of the illuminated part are visible. The phases of the moon can be explained by this experiment. Half of the moon is lighted by the sun; all of the illuminated half that is turned towards the earth is seen bright; the moon moves round the earth and turns different parts to it at different times.

ASTRONOMY

But we are on the earth, and the bright part of the moon is not always turned towards us. We see only so much of the bright part as *is* turned towards us—so much and no more.

Agnes. Sometimes we see the whole circle of the moon bright—at *full moon*.

Jack. Yes, we see it so when the sun is setting in the west and the moon rising in the east. The sun is shining full on the moon, and the bright half of the moon is turned full towards us.

Tom. When the moon is a sickle it is often in the west, not far from the sun about sunset.

Jack. That is the phase we call *new moon*.

Tom. The moon goes round the earth, doesn't it?

Jack. It goes round the earth once in every month. The moon's month begins when the moon is a *new moon*. Every night the bright part gets larger, and in about a week, a quarter of a month, we see a quarter of the moon bright; that is the *first quarter*. Two weeks after the new moon the full moon comes; and a week later comes a moon that is only partly bright again; that is the *third quarter*. By and by, in four weeks, comes another new moon, and so on forever.

Agnes. One of my storybooks says the old moons are cut up to make stars out of. They wouldn't be bright enough, would they?

Jack. Not exactly. Stars are the brightest things there are except the sun, which is the very brightest thing we know.

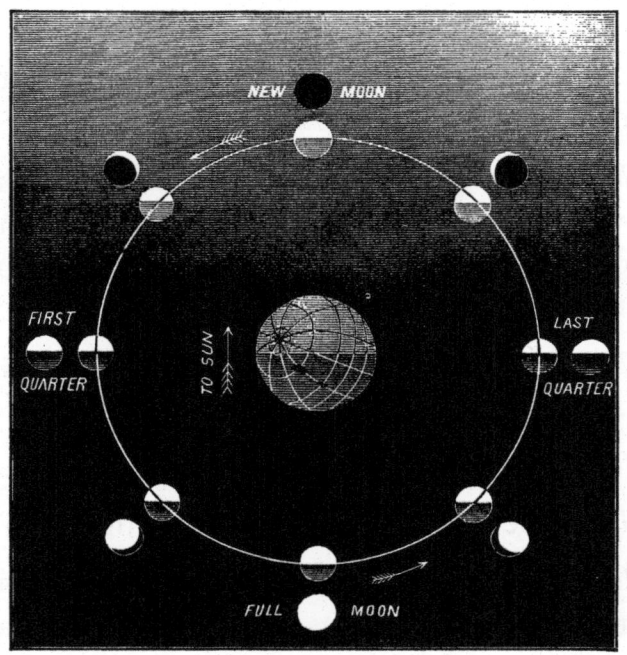

FIGURE 26

This picture shows why the moon's disk has different shapes at different times. The sun is supposed to be far away in the direction of the top of the page. It shines on the earth and lights half of it. It is night on the unlighted half of the earth. The moon goes around the earth in its orbit in the direction of the arrow. Wherever the moon is, one half of it is lighted—the half turned towards the sun. A person on the earth sees one half of the moon—the half turned towards him. The little circles *outside* the orbit in the picture show the shape that the bright part of the moon will have at new moon, full moon, etc.

Agnes. There are faint stars, though—some that you can scarcely see.

Tom. They are faint only because they are far off. If you were near them, they would be bright like the sun.

Jack. That's right. The stars are suns, and our sun is a star. All of them are really very much alike, though the stars do not look at all as the sun does. The sun looks large, and it is hot, because it is close to us. The stars look small because they are so far off, and we get no heat at all from them, though we get light. You know you can see the light of a lamp much farther than you can feel its heat.

Number of the Stars.—*Agnes.* There are thousands and thousands of stars, Jack; do you know how many there are?

Jack. There are about 6000 stars that you can see with the naked eye, not more; and you cannot see all those at once. Probably you never see more than a couple of thousands at any one time.

Agnes. Why, there seem to be many more than 2000.

Jack. Well, my dear, the only way to know is to count them. And the astronomers *have* counted them, and made maps that show every one of them by a little dot. That is the way they know how many there are. But if you take an opera glass, you can see very many more; and if you take a telescope, you can see thousands and thousands. The largest telescopes that we have will show

THE SCIENCES

FIGURE 27 THE GROUP OF STARS CALLED THE PLEIADES

The six brightest stars can be seen with the naked eye. To see the others a small telescope must be used. The Pleiades may be seen high up in the sky and to the south of the point overhead about 10 P.M. December 21, about 9 P.M. January 5, about 8 P.M. January 20, every year. Or you may see them rising to the north of the east point of your horizon about 10 P.M. August 23, about 9 P.M. September 8, about 8 P.M. September 23.

perhaps a hundred million stars. The brightest stars are nearest to us, and the faint ones are very far away indeed—inconceivably far, in fact.

Tom. You said the nearest star was as far away from the sun on our map as New York is from Peking. Are all the stars as far apart as that? Aren't some of them close together?

Clusters of Stars.—*Jack.* Well, there are some groups of stars fairly close together; but generally one star is about as far from the star nearest to it as our sun is from the nearest star. If you were making a map of the whole universe, you would begin by making a model of the solar system just as you did yesterday. The library globe would stand for the sun, which is one of the stars, you know. The nearest star to it would be shown on the map by a globe set down at Peking, 8000 miles away from us, and 8000 miles from Peking there would be another globe, and 8000 miles farther another one, and so on. Every 8000 miles on your map there would be a globe to stand for a star, and there would be at least a hundred million globes on your map of the universe, because, you know, the telescopes show us at least a hundred million stars. Of course these stars are scattered all around us; they aren't in a straight line one after another, but they are scattered all over the surface of the night sky.

Agnes. The planets move around the sun; do the stars move around the sun, too?

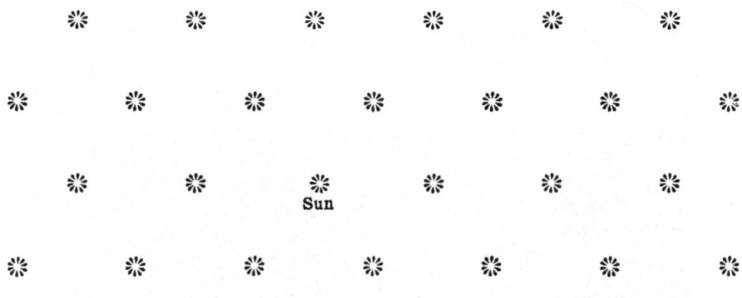

FIGURE 28

The stars in space are arranged somewhat as in the picture. On the whole, no one of them is nearer to any other one than the sun is to the nearest star,—20,000,000,000,000 miles. The sun is just one out of a countless number of stars—one out of millions. No one of the planets of the solar system can be seen from the nearest of the stars.

Jack. No, they are so far off from us that the sun has nothing to do with them, nor they with the sun. The sun has its own family of planets, and it is possible that the stars—which are suns—have their own planets, too; but we do not know whether they have or not.

Agnes. Why don't you know, Jack?

Jack. Because the stars are so far away. We can see

the stars like bright shining points in the sky. They shine by their own light and are bright. Now suppose any one of the stars really had a family of planets around it. Those planets would shine by the light from that star, and they would be faint, much too faint for us to see, even if the planets were really there; and the only way to know about stars and planets is to see them; you cannot touch them or hear them. If you cannot see a planet it does not exist, so far as you know.

Tom. Couldn't a man on the nearest star, looking at our sun, see the planets of our system,—Venus and Jupiter?

FIGURE 29

A photograph of a part of the Milky Way. Each little dot in the picture is a star, and there are thousands of them even on one photographic plate. You can see the Milky Way like a bright belt in the sky—a belt made of stars—overhead early in the evenings of August and September or of November, December, and January, or parallel to the northern horizon early in the evenings of April and May.

Jack. No, indeed; he would see our sun, but the light of our planets would be too faint. He could not possibly see them.

FIGURE 30 THE STARLIT SKY

Do the Stars have Planets as the Sun does?—*Tom.* You say you don't *know* whether the stars have planets round them. What do you *think* about it? Haven't you any idea?

Jack. There is a great deal of difference between knowing and thinking. I certainly do not know that the stars have planets, for I have never seen them. But I do think that it is very likely that they have families of planets, just as the sun has. I think it is likely—very likely; but I don't know.

Tom. And do you think those planets, if there are

any, have people on them? Are they inhabited as the earth is?

Jack. That is a hard question. In the first place, it is not certain that there are any planets around the stars, and then it is a mere guess whether there could be inhabitants on them. That is one of the questions we shall have to give up. It is too difficult.

Agnes. I am going to believe that every star has planets round it, just as the sun has.

Jack. Well, that is reasonable enough. Very likely you are right. Who knows?

Agnes. And I am going to believe that some of these planets round the stars have men on them.

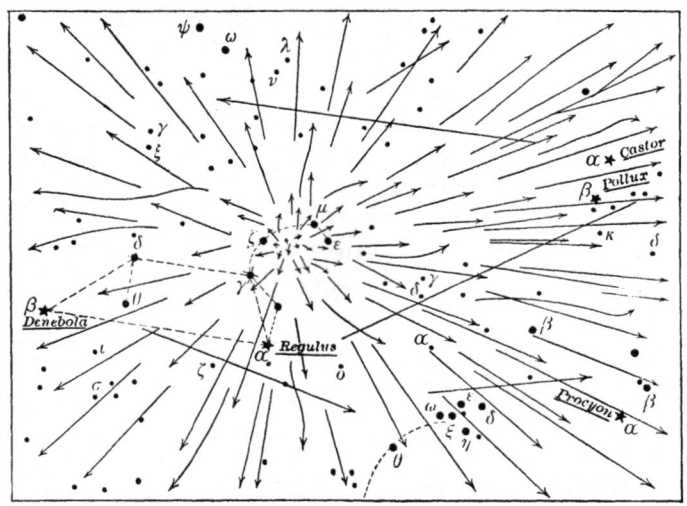

FIGURE 31 THE SHOWER OF SHOOTING STARS SEEN ON NOV. 13, 1866

The round dots stand for *stars;* the arrows for the tracks of meteors that were seen. Notice that nearly all the meteors radiated from a spot near the center of the picture.

Jack. I can't say you're wrong; I can't prove that you are wrong. Who knows? You can believe what you like about it. Wait till we know more.

FIGURE 32 THE GREAT METEOR THAT FELL IN CALIFORNIA IN 1894

Shooting Stars; Meteors; Fireballs.—On the night of August 10 the children stayed up late to watch the shooting stars that are regularly seen every year on that particular night. On almost any night that is clear any one who will watch for an hour will see a dozen or more; and the easiest way to understand what they are like is to watch for them. In the country, where the sky is dark

THE SCIENCES

and where there are no electric lights, it is not hard to see them. In the city it is not so simple; the sky is too bright and the street lamps interfere too much. Any one can see the stars. If one of the stars should suddenly get brighter and move quickly away from its place and then suddenly disappear, as if it had been blown out like a candle, it would look just as the shooting stars do. The real stars stay in the same place night after night, year after year, century after century. They are called *fixed* stars because they are fixed in their places. The shooting stars are small pieces of stone or iron that are moving about in space, as the planets move. One of these pieces comes near to the earth and falls to the ground just as a stone falls. It moves rapidly through the air and gets hot, as your hand will get hot if you move it very rapidly to and fro on your desk. The shooting star moves very fast and gets very hot indeed—hot enough to burn. Usually the meteors (shooting stars) get so hot in their flight through the air that they are quite burned up before they reach the ground. Sometimes a piece of iron falls and is picked up. The picture shows a piece of the sort.

FIGURE 33 A METEORIC STONE THAT FELL IN IOWA IN 1875

Figure 32 shows how such a meteor (a very large one—much large than a shooting star) looks as it is falling.

FIGURE 34 THE ZODIACAL LIGHT
The best time to see it in the United States is in February, March, and April in the early evening, above the western horizon.

The Zodiacal[1] Light.—Space is full of such meteors, most of them small, like dust. The sun shines on them, and you can often see a triangle of faint light or glow, which is called the *zodiacal light*. If you live in the country, where the sky is dark, be on the lookout for it. The street lamps of the city make the sky entirely too bright for you to see it in towns.

[1] Pronounced zō-dī′a-kal

Nebulæ.—*Nebula*, in Latin, means cloud; and nebulæ is the plural. There are several spots in the sky that, even with the naked eye, on a clear night look as if the stars in those spots were covered with a thin veil of cloud. When these spots are looked at with a telescope you see bright forms like those in the pictures Figures 35 and 53, and they are, in fact, bright clouds of gas and small particles of dust. They shine by their own light.

Figure 35 The Great Nebula in Andromeda, from a Photograph made with a Telescope (see Figure 53)

ASTRONOMY

FIGURE 36 THE SETTING SUN

Rising and Setting of the Sun.—*Tom*. We know that the sun rises in the east every day—

Agnes. And goes across the sky and sets in the west.

Jack. Why does it? Does the sun really move?

Agnes. No; the earth turns round and the sun stands still; but the sun *seems* to move.

Jack. The sun seems to move across the sky from rising to setting every day; the moon does the same thing; each one of the thousands of stars rises and then sets every night. There are just two ways to explain these things. Either the earth stands still and all these different heavenly bodies really move around it—every one of them—in twenty-four hours, or the heavenly bodies stand still and the earth turns round on its axis every day. The last explanation is the true one, as you know very well, and so we have to say the sun *appears* to move from rising to setting (for the sun really does not move at all); and we have to say the stars *appear* to move from rising to setting (for the stars do not really move at all). It is the earth that turns, and as it turns everything in the sky *appears* to move from east to west.

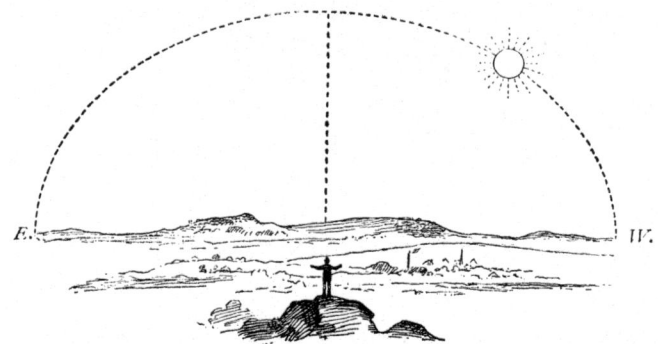

Figure 37   The Way the Sun seems to move from Rising to Setting

The man in the picture is looking towards the south, and his arms are stretched out to the east and to the west. If he stood there all day, he would see the sun rise above the horizon in the east, gradually rise higher and higher and be highest at noon, just to the south, and then decline towards the west and set in the west at the end of the day. The dotted line shows the apparent motion of the sun. The picture was drawn at about three o'clock in the afternoon. Why? Because the sun in the picture is where the real sun will be every day about three o'clock.

The Celestial Sphere.—"Think of it this way. You are on a globe—the earth—that turns around every twenty-four hours. Above you is the sky. It looks exactly as if it were a hollow globe, and as if you were inside of it. In the night-time the stars look like little shining marks fastened to the hollow globe all around you. In the daytime the sun (and sometimes the moon) seems to be fastened to the inside of the hollow globe of the sky. We call the hollow globe of the sky the *celestial sphere*. You are in the middle of it, and you see all the stars at night slowly moving from rising towards setting. The celestial sphere is the surface of the sky to which the sun, moon, and stars appear to be fastened. They look as if they were fastened there, anyway. They all seem to be at the same distance."

Tom. They can't all be fastened to any one sphere,

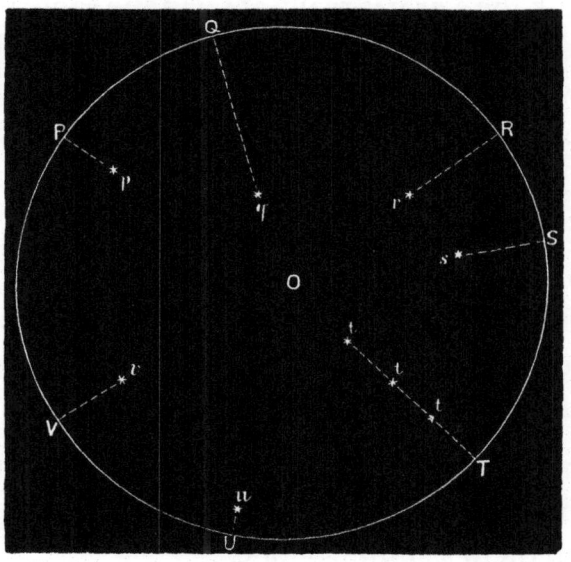

FIGURE 38 THE CELESTIAL SPHERE
(THE HOLLOW GLOBE ON WHOSE INNER SURFACE ALL STARS SEEMS TO LIE)

The earth is supposed to be at *O*, and some stars at *p, q, r, s, t, t, t, u, v*. You see the stars as if they were all projected on the celestial sphere at *P, Q, R, S, T, U, V*. You think of them as if they were all at the same distance from you.

because they are at very different distances from us. The sun is very much further away from us than the moon, and the stars are much further off than the sun.

Jack. True enough. If you will look at this picture I am drawing, you will see how it is. You are supposed to be in the middle of the celestial sphere at O. The earth is at O (Figure 38), and you are on it. All around you are stars, *p, q, r, s,* etc. You see the star *q* along the line O*q*—along the line that joins your eye and the star. The line seems to pierce the celestial sphere at Q, and you think the star *q* is really at Q. In the same way you think the star *r* is at R, the star *s* at S, and so forth. If there were really three stars, *t, t, t,* all in one line, O*t*, you would see only one star at T. All the stars seem to be lying on the surface of some sphere, and all of them seem equally far away.

Tom. That is true, I know. When I look at the stars at night they certainly do seem to be all at one distance—just like shining tacks driven into a darkish globe above my head and all around me.

Agnes. And in the daytime the sun and, sometimes, the moon seem to be the same way—shining circles fastened on to a shining globe.

Jack. Of course there isn't any real globe there. It is only an appearance. But it looks real, and we have a name for the appearance because it is convenient to have names for things we always see, or even for things that we always think that we see.

Tom. You would have a model of the celestial sphere by making a huge hollow globe as big as a barn and

FIGURE 39

This picture shows the northern sky as it appears in the early hours of the evening every August to people who live in the United States. If you face north, you see the *horizon*—the surface of the ground. Above that comes the sky with many stars in it. Towards the west and pretty high up is the Dipper—the Great Bear (Ursa Major). Two of its stars—the pointers—point at the north star—Polaris, it is called. High in the east is Cassiopeia, a group that is sometimes called The Lady in the Chair. Every child that owns this book should try to find these stars. They are always there, in the north. If he looks in August they will be just as in the picture. If he looks in other months the book must be turned a little. By taking a little pains the book can be held so that the picture will look as the stars do.

getting inside of it.

Agnes. Yes, and by lining it with black velvet and driving bright-headed tacks into the lining for stars; only you would have to drive them in the right places.

Jack. A model like that would be worth making, but it would be expensive. We shall have to do with pictures and flat maps. They will explain what we really see in the sky.

The next night Jack took the children out of doors. He made them face towards the north; the east was on their right hand, the west on their left. First of all he showed them the Dipper—the Great Bear (*Ursa Major* in Latin)—and the pointers.

FIGURE 40 THE DIPPER—THE GREAT BEAR—AS IT APPEARS AT DIFFERENT TIMES

Sometimes it is above the pole, sometimes below it; but if you lay ruler on the picture, you will see that the pointers always point to the north star—Polaris.

The Dipper is made up of seven bright stars and is always easy to find. Three of its stars make the handle, four make the bowl, and two stars of the bowl are the pointers. After you have found the pointers it is easy to find the polestar. Now if you imagine a line drawn from the polestar to the center of the earth (under your feet), that line will be the axis of the earth. The earth turns round that line every day. Every part of the axis itself stands still, and every point not in the axis moves. The center of the earth stands still while the earth turns; and Polaris stands still. All the parts of the earth not on the axis appear to move, and all the stars except Polaris appear to move—they move from rising to setting and back to rising again. The stars in the east move upwards, then over the pole towards the west, and then downwards (in the direction of the little arrows in Figures 39 and 40).

Jack kept the children out of doors till long after their bedtime to let them see the stars rise higher and higher, but finally they had to go to bed. They could not watch any longer.

On the next night Jack showed the children how the southern stars appeared to move from rising to setting. He took them out into a large open field and made them face towards the south. The east was on their left hand, the west on their right hand, and the stars appeared to move from east to west,—from rising towards setting—just as the sun does. The apparent motion of all the stars—of the south stars as well as of the north stars—is caused by one thing and one thing only. The earth turns round on its axis underneath the starry sky.

THE SCIENCES

Time and Timekeeping.—We use the apparent motion of the sun from rising to setting to give us the time. Watches and clocks all over the world are now regulated by the sun. Long ago the ancients used to tell their time by the stars. They would say: "You must begin your

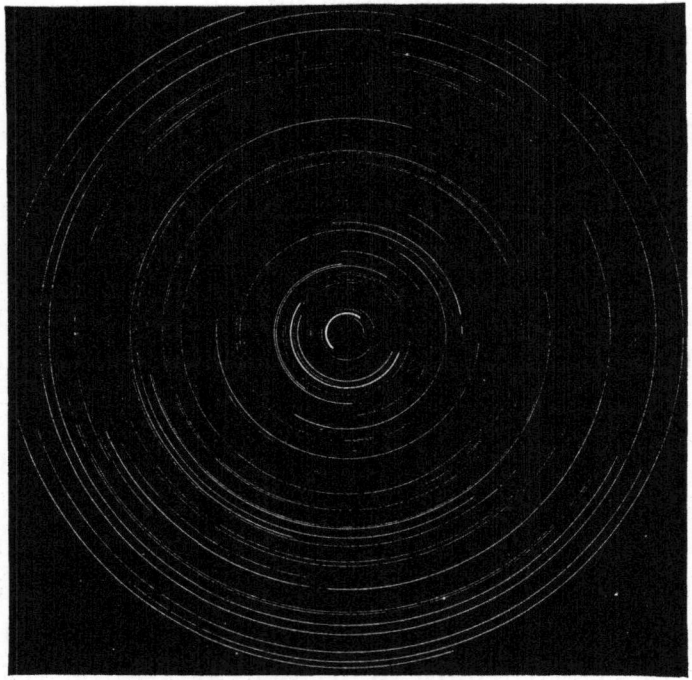

FIGURE 41

A photograph of a part of the northern sky near the pole. A camera was pointed at the pole early in the evening and the plate was exposed all night and only shut off at daybreak. Each star moved about half of its course round the pole, and as it moved it left a *trail* on the plate. All the trails in the picture are half circles. The star Polaris is not *exactly* at the north pole of the heavens (though it happens to be pretty near it). Its trail is the brightest one on the plate. The other stars left their trails, too.

ASTRONOMY

FIGURE 42

A photograph of a part of the southern sky, showing the *trails* of southern stars as they moved across the plate from rising towards setting. This photograph, and the one like it for the northern stars, prove that the stars really move with respect to the photographic plate. But it is not the stars that move. The plate moves with the earth as the earth turns round its axis. The stars stand still.

journey when Pleiades are rising"; just as we might say: "I must take the train at 9 P.M." Groups of stars, like the Pleiades, were the moving clock hands; the dial was the celestial sphere. The stars moved steadily across the dial, and their motion told the hour. The sun moves regularly and steadily from rising to setting. When it is highest up in the heavens and exactly south of any place (a city, a town, *any* place), then it is *noon* at that particular place. Twelve hours later it is *midnight*; and twelve hours later than midnight it is noon again—noon of the next day of

THE SCIENCES

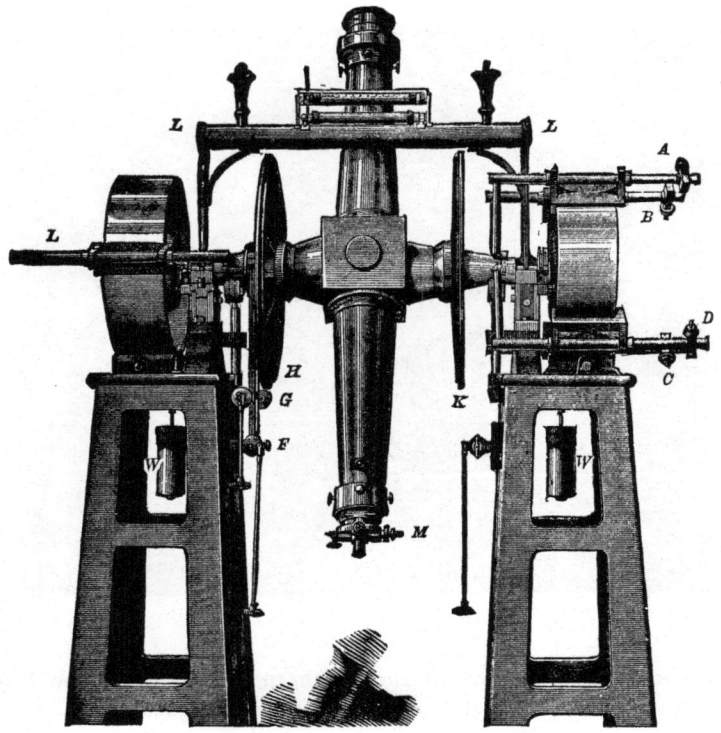

FIGURE 43 A MERIDIAN CIRCLE

The eye end of the telescope is at *M*. The telescope is fastened to a horizontal axis which lies in an east and west line, and the telescope always remains, therefore, in the meridian. *LL* is a level by which the axis is made horizontal. The axis has two circles (*H* and *K*) fastened to it. These circles are divided into 360 degrees, and by them we can measure the altitude (height), of any star.

the week. A watch is a little machine arranged to drive a steel hand round a dial in twelve hours. The hand is set so as to mark XII o'clock at noon, and the machine is regulated so that when the next noon comes the hand shall be at XII again. To set our watches *exactly*, we must have a north and south line. Astronomers have a particular kind of telescope set exactly in the north and

ASTRONOMY

south line (the *meridian*), so that they can observe the exact instant of noon. Their watches are corrected so as to mark XII o'clock just at that moment; and made to run so that when the next noon comes they will mark XII o'clock again. They have other kinds of telescopes also, especially made to examine distant planets and to discover what is to be seen on their surfaces.

Telescopes.—The children were playing with a reading glass that belonged to their father. Tom used it to light a match with, and then to look at the wings of a fly, and noticed how it magnified everything—how it made it look much larger.

Figure 44
A Reading Glass, a Magnifying Lens, or a Burning Glass

Then he said: "Jack, what is the difference between this magnifying glass and a telescope? Both of them magnify."

Jack. Well, the telescope magnifies very much more, for one thing; and a telescope is made up of more than one lens. The burning glass has only one.

Jack took the burning glass and showed the children how to use it to make an image (a picture) of the window on the wall, as in Figure 45.

Jack. You see that this glass makes an image of the window on the wall. Suppose that we should cut a hole in the wall just where the image is now. The image would be there just the same, for if you put a piece of white paper over the hole the image would show on the paper as it now does on the wall. Now suppose that you were in the other room beyond the wall and held another burning glass in just the right place to magnify the image in the hole. The second burning glass magnifies everything it looks at; well, you could use it to magnify the image formed by the first burning glass. If you did this, you would have a telescope. Two lenses combined so as to form a magnified image of any object make a telescope. One lens alone is not a telescope; it is a magnifying glass.

Agnes. Then a telescope must have two glasses?

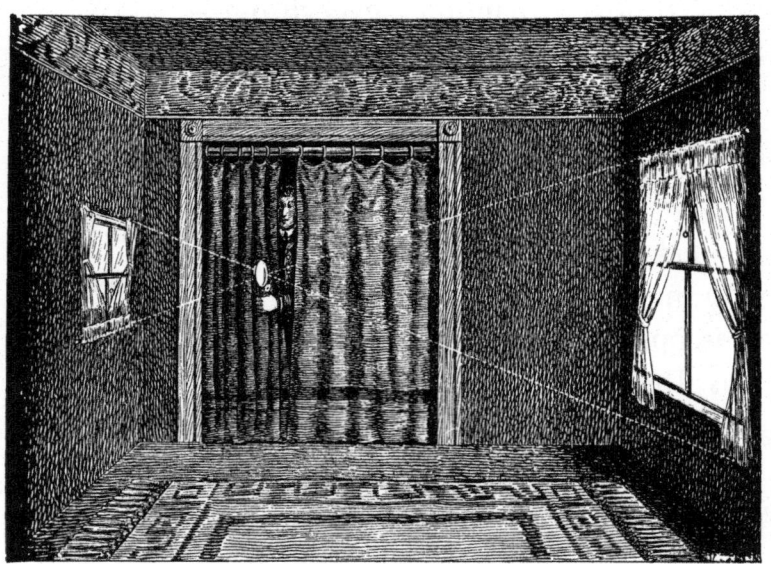

FIGURE 45

If you hold a burning glass in a room, you can make it form an image (a picture) of the window on the opposite wall. The image will be clear and distinct, but it will be upside down, as you can prove by trying. Most lenses will need to be held nearer the wall than that in the figure.

Jack. Yes, two at least; the first glass forms an image of the thing you are looking at—a picture of the window, for instance. The second glass magnifies the image so that you can see it better and see it larger. All opera glasses and spyglasses have at least two lenses, usually more than two.

Tom. Here is a drawing of the great telescope of the Lick Observatory (Figure 46). Where are the two glasses there?

Jack. One of them is the upper end of the long steel tube; they call it the *object glass,* because it is nearest the object you are lookng at. The other glass is at the other end of the tube; they call it the *eyepiece,* because it is next your eye. In the drawing you see a man looking through the eyepiece.

Agnes. But the telescope is inside a house, Jack. How can the astronomer see anything?

Tom. Why, you know, Agnes, that there is a long window in the dome that is opened when they want to look out to see anything. The telescope looks out through the open window.

Agnes. What is the long tube for?

Jack. It is principally to keep the object glass and the eyepiece at exactly the right distance apart and to hold them steadily where you want them.

Tom. The tube is on an iron stand, and you can go to the top of the stand by a winding stairway. What are those big circles at the top, Jack?

Jack. The circles are fastened to the telescope, Tom,

FIGURE 46 THE GREAT TELESCOPE
OF THE LICK OBSERVATORY

Its object glass is three feet in diameter, and it is nearly sixty feet long.

not to the iron stand, you see; and they are arranged to show the latitude and the longitude of the particular star that the telescope is pointed at.

Agnes. Do they know the latitudes and the longitudes of stars?

Jack. Yes, that is the way they point at them. If I tell you to find on the map a town that has a latitude of 41 degrees and a longitude of 80 degrees you can find it, can't you?

Agnes. Here is the map, and the town is Pittsburg.

Jack. Well, the astronomers have maps of the stars, and they find the star they want by knowing its latitude and longitude, and by pointing the telescope there.

Tom. But the star would be moving from rising to setting. How do they manage to follow it?

Jack. If you will look at the drawing of the telescope (Figure 46), you'll see a piece of machinery in the top part of the stand. It is really a powerful clock. That clock is arranged so as to move the telescope towards the west exactly as fast as the star moves toward the west. When you once have the star in the telescope the clock keeps it there.

Agnes. How large is the object glass of the Lick telescope?

Jack. The object glass is three feet in diameter, and the tube is nearly sixty feet long, and the eyepiece is quite small—just the size to be convenient for your eye to see through, Agnes.

Tom. How much can you magnify with a telescope like that?

The Moon.—*Jack.* Well, you can arrange so as to magnify more or less as you please. For instance, you can magnify the moon about a thousand times—you can see the moon as if it were a thousand times nearer than it really is. How far off did I tell you the moon is?

Tom. Two hundred and forty thousand miles.

Jack. Then if the telescope will make it seem a thousand times nearer, how far off will it seem to be?

Agnes. Two hundred and forty miles.

Jack. That's right, my dear. The Lick telescope will show you the moon just as you would see it if you got within two hundred and forty miles of it—just as if the moon were at Pittsburg and you at Philadelphia.

Agnes. That does not seem very near.

Jack. Well, it isn't near; but it is wonderful to do even so well as that.

Tom. Then the planets, that are so

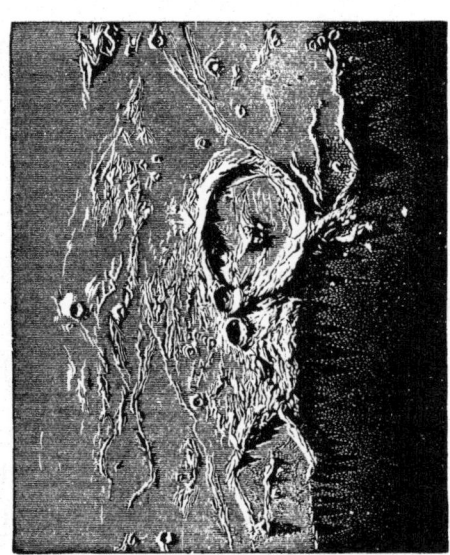

FIGURE 47 MOUNTAINS ON THE MOON, AS SEEN IN A TELESCOPE

much farther away than the moon, cannot be seen anything like so well?

Jack. No; Mars, for instance, is 50,000,000 miles away from us when we see it best, and so we never can make it seem nearer to us than 50,000 miles. That is better than nothing; but it isn't very close, after all. It is really wonderful that men have found out so much as they have about the planets when you consider what the difficulties are. The smallest spot that can be seen with distinctness on the moon would contain several acres; and when you come to looking at a distant planet like Mars a spot would have to be fifty or sixty miles square to be visible at all.

Tom. Then you might see a city on the moon? A city covers many acres.

Jack. You could see a city on the moon if it were there; or even a *very* large building like the Capitol at Washington; but

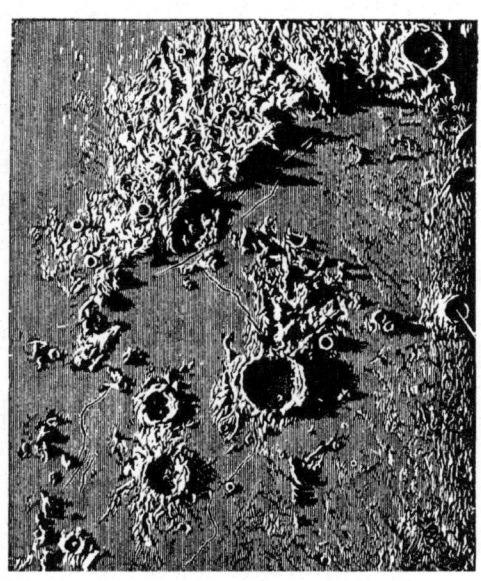

FIGURE 48 MOUNTAINS ON THE MOON, AS SEEN IN A TELESCOPE

there are no such cities or buildings on the moon. Astronomers have looked for them thousands of times without ever finding the slightest sign of any living thing.

THE SCIENCES

Life on the Planets.—*Agnes*. Is there any sign of life on the planets?

Jack. Not one; life of some sort may be there—plants, trees, animals, or possibly men—but the telescope shows no sign of life at all.

Tom. Not even on Mars?

Jack. Not even on Mars—nowhere. Some people have talked about land and water on Mars, calling parts of Mars that are reddish, land, and parts that are bluish, water; but no one has any proof at all that the red parts are really land, or the blue parts water.

Tom. I have read about canals in Mars.

Jack. Well, whatever they are, they are not canals. The telescope shows narrow, straight, dark lines on the planet's surface (see Figure 49), and they were called *canals* because they crossed the red parts of Mars that were called *continents*. But the Lick telescope shows that the canals go across the oceans, just as they go across the continents; so that it is pretty clear that the canals are not canals at all, and that we do not know whether Mars has any water on its surface at all.

Tom. How is it about Jupiter?

Jack. Jupiter looks as if it were a very hot planet; like a huge red-hot ball covered with clouds of steam. All of Saturn that we can see seems to be clouds; and the same is true for Uranus and Neptune, and for Venus, too, for that matter. Mercury and Mars have no clouds and probably little or no atmosphere at all. All the others have atmospheres, but no one knows whether their air is the right kind of air to breathe. It is very doubtful whether any planet beside the earth is fit for men to live on.

Tom. Is there air on the moon?

Jack. There is no air on the moon at all, nor any water either; and it is so cold on the moon, and on Mars too, that no man could possibly live there for an instant.

Tom. Then there isn't any place in the whole universe where we are really sure that men can live except just the earth?

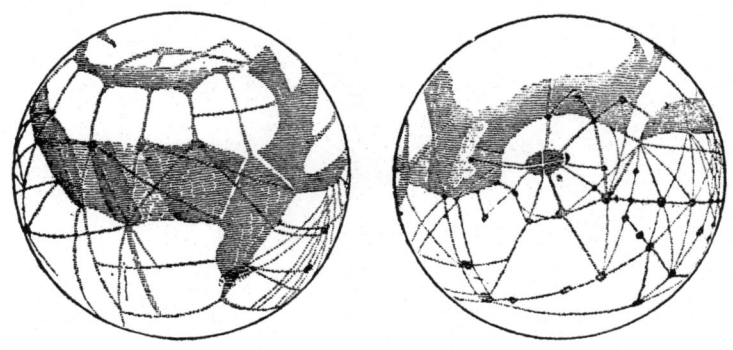

FIGURE 49

Drawings showing two hemispheres of the planet Mars. The narrow lines are what have been called *canals*. The dark parts of the drawing should be colored blue and most of the white parts reddish in order to make it look as Mars does.

Jack. No. Men cannot live in the sun; the sun is too hot. Jupiter is too hot, also. Mercury and Mars have little or no air. Venus, Saturn, and Uranus, and Neptune are covered with clouds, and we do not know what is underneath the clouds. Men couldn't live in the stars;

they are like the sun—too hot. And we do not know whether the stars have planets round them or not; very likely they have. If they have, some of their planets may be fit for men to live on. Agnes says she is going to believe it.

Agnes. Yes, I am. It makes the universe more interesting to believe that there are people like ourselves everywhere, or at least in many places.

Jack. Well, believe it, my dear. I half believe it myself; but there is no way to prove it, or to disprove it, for that matter.

APPENDIX

The Earth

The earth is a globe flattened at the poles. Its shortest diameter (from pole to pole) is 7900 miles. Its longest diameter is 7927 miles. It turns on its axis once daily. It moves in its orbit round the sun once in a year of 365 days 5 hours 48 minutes 45 ½ seconds. Its *month* (from new moon to new moon) is 29 ½ days. The earth is 5 ½ times as heavy as a globe of water of the same size. The sun weighs 333,000 times more than the earth. The distance from the earth to the sun is 93,000,000 miles.

The Moon

The moon is 2163 miles in diameter. The moon weighs about 3 ½ times as much as a globe of water of the same size. The earth weighs 81 times as much as the moon. The distance from the moon to the earth is 240,000 miles.

Eclipses of the Sun and Moon

They are explained in Physics.

The Planet Mercury

Mercury is 3030 miles in diameter. It weighs about 3 1/8 times as much as a globe of water of the same size. It goes once round the sun every 88 days. It is 36,000,000 miles distant from the sun—less than 4/10 of the earth's distance, therefore.

THE SCIENCES

THE PLANET VENUS

Venus is 7700 miles in diameter (about the size of the earth, therefore). It weighs 4 8/10 times as much as a globe of water of the same size. It goes round the sun once every 225 days. It is 67,200,000 miles distant from the sun—about 7/10 of the earth's distance, therefore.

FIGURE 50
A rough drawing of the full moon.

THE PLANET MARS

Mars is 4230 miles in diameter. It weighs 4 times as much as a globe of water of the same size. It turns once on its axis in 24 hours 37 minutes 22 67/100 seconds. It goes round the sun once every 687 days. It is 141,500,000 miles from the sun—about 1 ½ times the earth's distance, therefore. It has two very small moons.

ASTRONOMY

Jupiter

Jupiter is 86,500 miles in diameter. It weighs only 1 3/10 times as much as a globe of water of the same size. It turns once on its axis in 9 hours 55 minutes. It goes round the sun once every 11 9/10 years. It is 483,300,000 miles from the sun—about 5 times the earth's distance, therefore. It has nine moons. Five of them are very small; the others much larger—about the size of our own moon, or of the planet Mars.

The Planet Saturn

Saturn is made up of a globe with rings around it. The diameter of its globe is 73,000 miles. It weighs only 7/10 as much as a globe of water of the same size. The globe turns on its axis every 10 hours 14 minutes 24 seconds. It goes round the sun once every 29 ½ years. It is 886,000,000 miles distant from the sun—about 9 ½ times the earth's distance, therefore.

The *rings* of Saturn are made up of a swarm of countless little moons. The rings are about 28,000 miles wide and 168,000 miles in diameter, and only about 100 miles thick. Saturn has nine moons—one as large as Mars, one about the size of our moon, and the rest smaller.

The Planet Uranus

Uranus is 31,900 miles in diameter. It weighs only 1 2/10 as much as a globe of water of the same size. It goes round the sun once in 84 years. It is 1,781,900,000 miles distant from the sun—about 19 times as far as

THE SCIENCES

FIGURE 51   THE SUN AT TOTAL ECLIPSE
The black circle is the disk of the moon; behind it the sun's disk is hidden. The pale white light is the sun's *corona*, or crown. The corona always surrounds the sun, but is not visible every day because it is so faint.

the earth, therefore. It has four rather small moons. It turns on its axis every 10 hours 50 minutes.

THE PLANET NEPTUNE

Neptune is 34,800 miles in diameter. It weighs only 1 1/10 times as much as a globe of water of the same size. It goes round the sun once in 165 years. It is 2,791,600,000 miles distant from the sun—about 30 times the earth's distance, therefore. It has one moon about the size of our own moon.

Comets

A few comets belong to the family of the sun and move around him as do the planets.

The Fixed Stars

Stars are suns, immensely distant from our sun and from each other except when they are grouped in *clusters*. Light, which travels nearly 200,000 miles in a *second*, takes 4 *years* to come to us from the nearest star. The light from *Polaris* (the polestar) takes 47 years to reach the earth. Many stars are millions of times as large as the earth and may give off 1000 times as much light as our sun.

Nebulæ

Nebulæ are masses of gas at about the same distance from the sun as the stars are. They are of all shapes and sizes. Many of them are spiral in shape—corkscrew shaped. If, as sometimes happens, a star burns up it may turn into a nebula; or, as sometimes happens, a nebula may solidify and become a star. Perhaps our sun and all the planets were once a huge nebula that cooled and solidified into separate globes.

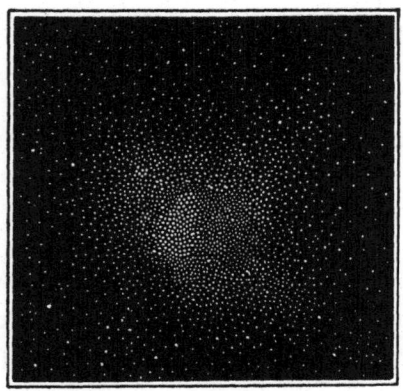

FIGURE 52 A CLUSTER OF STARS IN THE CONSTELLATION OF THE CENTAUR

Each white dot represents a star.

FIGURE 53

Drawing of a large nebula (in Andromeda) as seen in a telescope. The white dots are stars; the shining white cloud is the nebula. (See also Figure 35)

PHYSICS

THE SCIENCE THAT EXPLAINS HEAT, LIGHT, SOUND, ELECTRICITY, MAGNETISM

Solids and Liquids.—"What is the difference between a solid and a liquid?" said Tom one hot afternoon when the children were all together on the porch, fanning themselves.

Mary. You can pick up a solid with your fingers, and you cannot pick up a liquid—that's one difference.

Agnes. You mean you can pick up a piece of ice, and you cannot pick it up when it has melted into water?

Mary. Of course you can't.

Fred. Oh, yes, you can—and with that Fred took a lump of sugar and put it in a teaspoon partly filled with water. The sugar took up the water, and Fred picked up the sugar and left the spoon quite empty, saying: "Look at that! I've picked up a liquid in my fingers. It's magic."

Agnes. That is just foolish, Fred.

Fred. I know it—but it is magic. You said I couldn't do it.

THE SCIENCES

Tom. It isn't fair, Fred; you can pick up a sponge with water in it, but you cannot pick up the water without the sponge, nor the water without the sugar, either.

Fred. All right. I was just playing. It *is* a kind of magic, though.

Mary. Well, wasn't I right? A solid is a thing you can pick up in your fingers, and a liquid is something you can't pick up.

Tom. The real magic of it is that a piece of ice and a spoonful of water are just the same thing. The same thing is different at different times; sometimes it is ice, and sometimes water. I wonder why. Let us ask Jack.

Jack. I think Mary's definition is a pretty good one—a solid is a thing you can pick up in your fingers. You can change a solid into a liquid, if you want to, by heating it. You can change a piece of ice into water by letting it melt. A little heat will do it.

Fred. How does heat do it, Jack?

FIGURE 54

A solid, a piece of iron for instance, is made up of thousands and thousands of little particles, each one like every other one, all crowded together like the lower part of the picture. When you heat a solid the little particles are forced farther apart, so that by and by they look like the upper part of the picture. The solid will get larger if you heat it.

Solids, Liquids, and Gases are Made up of Millions of Small Particles.— *Jack.* Well, you have to begin far off if you wish to understand. The scientific men have proved that all solids—and all liquids too—are made up of little particles crowded close together. When you heat a solid the particles are forced farther and farther apart.

Heat makes Solids, etc., expand.—"A piece of solid iron gets larger when you heat it. When a blacksmith wants to fit a new tire on a wheel, he first heats it and puts it on; then the tire, as it gets cold again, shrinks tightly on the wheel and stays where it is put."

"Every little particle of the tire has been forced apart by the heat, and by and by the whole tire, which was in the first place smaller than the wheel, grows large enough to slip over the rim. Then the blacksmith slips it on and lets it cool. As it cools, it shrinks and fits the rim tightly. The heat has loosened the particles you might say."

Agnes. How do you know the particles are farther apart when the iron is hot?

Jack. There are just so many particles in the cold iron to begin with, Agnes—say ten millions of them, if you please. And you haven't put any more particles in the tire, you know; you have simply heated it. But the tire really has grown bigger—the proof is that it will slip over the rim of the wheel. The same ten million little particles of the cold iron fill a larger space than when they are cold; so they must have been forced farther

THE SCIENCES

FIGURE 55

The right-hand picture shows a wheel ready to be fitted with a tire; the middle picture shows the tire heated in a fire. When the tire has expanded—grown large—enough the blacksmith fits it on the wheel and lets it shrink tight by cooling.

apart somehow, you see. And the heat did it—nothing else could have done it.

Mary. Suppose you had heated the iron more and more, Jack. What then?

Jack. If you had put the iron in the furnace and kept on heating it, you would have had a hot solid at first; then it would have become pasty, almost like a dough, and by and by it would become a liquid—it would flow like water. You cannot try the experiment with iron, but you have often seen the boys try it with lead when they are molding bullets for their guns. Lead melts more quickly than iron.

Agnes. Yes, they put the lead in a ladle and melt it, and then pour it into molds and let it cool.

Jack. Iron is made up of one kind of small particles, and lead is made up of another kind of particles; and it takes less heat to separate the lead particles. But heat does the same thing always. It separates the particles farther, the more heat you apply. First you have a solid, and then a liquid; and if you heat the liquid enough, you have a gas—iron gas, lead gas.

Tom. If you were to go on heating iron gas for a week, what would you get? something different than gas?

Jack. No; you would get very hot iron gas and nothing more. You can have matter in only three forms—solid, liquid, gas—but you can turn one form into the other by heat or by cold. Take ice, for instance.

Fred. Ice is solid. If you make it colder and colder, it is nothing but ice—the north polar regions are ice and nothing else.

Agnes. And if you heat ice, it becomes water.

Mary. And if you heat water in a teakettle, it becomes steam.

Tom. And if you heat steam, Jack, more and more, is it always steam?

Jack. It is never anything else. It is simply very hot steam. The boiler of a locomotive or of a steamship makes steam and nothing else. Solid, liquid, gas—that is all you can get. If you cool a gas like steam *enough*, you will get a liquid; and if you cool a liquid *enough*, you will get a solid.

Most Gases are Invisible.—*Mary.* I have seen solids and liquids; but I'm not sure I have ever seen gases.

Fred. Well, you have smelled them, anyway, from leaky gas fixtures in the house, or when the match went out before you could light the gas at the burner.

Mary. Oh, yes; and of course, there is gas inside of the little toy balloons. But I have never seen gas.

Jack. Most gases cannot be seen. They are invisible. Air is invisible, but it is all around us. If any one asked you to prove that air was really all around us, Mary, how would you prove it?

Mary. Why, I should say that the wind was nothing but moving air.

Jack. That is a good idea, my dear. But suppose the wind wasn't blowing? Then what?

Mary. I should wait till it did.

Jack. You could make an experiment to prove it this way. Take an empty tumbler and hold it upside down. We call it empty, but it is really full of air—of invisible air. Then take a glass bowl half full of water and float a cork in it. Now gently press the tumbler down over the cork (see the picture) and see what you will see. If there were nothing in the tumbler—if the tumbler were really empty—then the water would fill it full; but you can see that the water rises only for a certain distance, and no higher. There is air in the

FIGURE 56

A glass bowl partly filled with water, a cork, and a glass tumbler are needed to prove that the tumbler was filled with air. This experiment should be tried in the classroom.

tumbler still.

Tom. I can prove that there is air in the tumbler now. Tip the tumbler sideways a little while it is in the bowl and the air will come out in bubbles.

Fred. What becomes of the air in the bubbles when they rise to the surface?

Tom. Why, it just mixes with the other air all around us.

The Diving Bell.—*Agnes.* The diving bell that men use at the bottom of rivers is like the tumbler, isn't it?

FIGURE 57 BUBBLES OF AIR ESCAPING FROM THE MOUTH OF A GOLDFISH IN A GLOBE

The Earth's Atmosphere.—*Jack.* The air is all around us everywhere, for wherever you go you find air to breathe.

Agnes. Not on the tops of mountains, Jack.

Jack. There is not so much air at the tops of mountains as there is below, Agnes, but there is air. Men have climbed the very highest mountains, and as they went up, they found less and less air. Birds fly nearly as high. The condor—a bird like an eagle—flies high in the Andes of South America, and balloons carrying men have gone seven miles high. A balloon without men has gone over twenty-one miles, but the air is so

FIGURE 58

The diving bell is lowered by a chain from a ship, and air is pumped into it by the pipe marked T in the picture. The whole diving bell is under water, but the water rises no higher than its floor. The pressure of the air keeps it out. The diver goes down to the bottom of the harbor and fastens ropes to whatever he wants to hoist to the surface. He has a waterproof and air-proof suit of clothes, and air is pumped down for him to breathe (through the small pipe in the picture). The foundations for the piers of bridges can be laid by men working in this way.

PHYSICS

FIGURE 59

The Himalaya Mountains are about five miles, and Mont Blanc, in the Alps, is about three miles above the level of the sea. A balloon carrying men has gone up five miles and very light balloons filled with gas have gone nearly ten miles above sea level.

thin at that height that men could not breathe.

Mary. The air gets thinner and thinner as you go up. Where does it stop then?

Jack. We do not know exactly; but it has been estimated all the way from 100 to 500 miles. These estimates are based on observations of the height at which meteors first become visible, and on the height of the aurora borealis.[1]

[1] See Astronomy, **Meteors**, page 47.

THE SCIENCES

Balloons.—*Tom.* The balloon floats in the air because it is lighter than the air, just as a chip floats on the water.

Mary. If the balloon is lighter than the air, then the air itself must be heavy; for a balloon weighs a good deal, especially when it is carrying men.

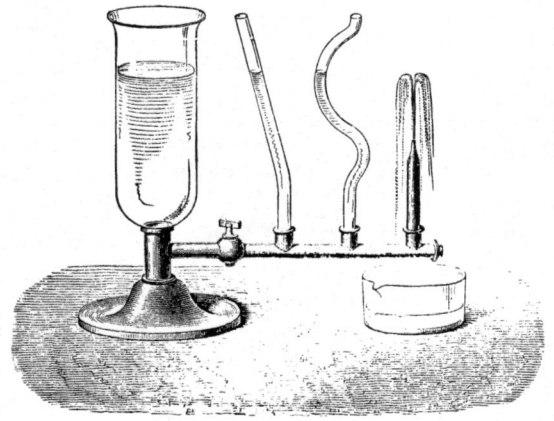

FIGURE 60

All these glass vessels are joined together by the brass tube at the bottom. If you fill the large jar at the left-hand side with water, all the other tubes will at once fill up to the same level. The air presses on the water in the large jar and forces it up into the other tubes and makes the little fountain play.

Air is Heavy.—*Jack.* Yes, the air is heavy, and there is a simple way to prove it.

Reservoirs, Fountains, and the Water Supplies of Cities.—"If you have a reservoir full of water and a

FIGURE 61   RESERVOIRS, FOUNTAINS, AND THE
WATER SUPPLY OF CITIES

The picture shows a lake which is the source from which the water is obtained. A dotted line across the picture marks the level of the upper surface of the lake. An aqueduct (water pipe) takes the water from the lake, carries it under the hill, under a pond, up another hill, where there is a fountain, and delivers the water to the city reservoir. From the city reservoir pipes conduct the water all over the city—to public fountains, to the upper stories of houses, and so forth. Notice that all the fountains send their jets to about the same height.

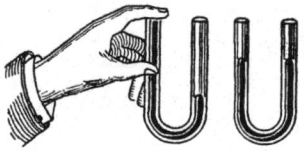

FIGURE 62

The U-shaped tube is partly filled with water as in the right-hand picture. Air fills the rest of both branches of the tube. Now tip the tube so that one branch of the tube shall be completely filled with water—water on one side, air on the other. Then cover the water side with your finger, as in the left-hand picture. You will see that the water will still stand at different heights on the two sides. There is air pressure on one side of the tube and no air pressure on the other (your finger keeps the air out). The air pressure keeps the water standing high. If you take your finger away and let the air in, the water on both sides of the tube will stand at the same level on both sides. (This experiment should be tried in the classroom.)

fountain joined to the reservoir by a pipe, the fountain will play as soon as the water is turned on, and the fountain will play as high[1] as the water in the reservoir. That is because the air above the reservoir is heavy and presses down on the water in it and forces it up in the fountain. (See Figure 61) Now here is an experiment that we can try ourselves with this bit of glass tube bent into the shape of a U.

"You can see that the air must be heavy; it must press down with weight because it makes the fountain play (Figure 61) and keeps the water standing high (Figure 62).

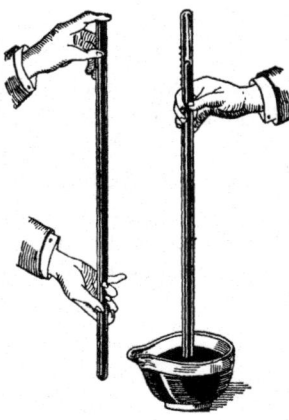

FIGURE 63
How to Make a Barometer
See the description in the text.

The Barometer.[2]—"Instead of using water in the U-shaped tubes, you can use any liquid—milk, kerosene oil, quicksilver. It is convenient to use quicksilver because it is heavy and because it is so clean.[3]

"You need a hollow glass tube about thirty-two inches long, closed at one end, a lot of

---

[1] Or nearly as high; the friction of the water in the pipe makes some difference.
[2] The barometer is an instrument to measure the weight—the pressure—of the air. The name comes from two Greek words, one meaning "weight" and the other "to measure."
[3] Quicksilver is a poison if taken in the mouth; it is perfectly safe to handle it unless there are cuts on the hands and fingers. If it touches a gold ring, however, it will cover the gold with a thin layer of quicksilver that will not wear off for some time.

PHYSICS

quicksilver, and a flat basin of glass or china. Hold the long tube with its open end upwards. It is full of air.

Make a paper funnel and pour quicksilver from a pitcher into the open tube, slowly and carefully, until you have quite filled it. As the quicksilver goes in it will drive out the air, and finally you will have a tube with *no* air in it—nothing but quicksilver. You must handle it carefully because it is quite heavy. Now put your finger over the open end of the long tube and turn the tube swiftly upside down. (See the left-hand picture, Figure 63.) If you should now take your finger away, all the quicksilver would fall out. There would be nothing to support it. But dip the open end of the long tube in the basin of quicksilver, take your finger away, and see what happens. The quicksilver will fall in the tube a little distance—a few inches—and then it will stop. The air is pressing on the quicksilver in the basin and is pressing some of it up into the tube. There is no air above the quicksilver in the tube; nothing is pressing downward except the weight of the quicksilver

FIGURE 64
A QUICKSILVER BAROMETER
READY FOR USE

The long glass tube has a scale of inches at the upper end; 28, 29, 30, 31 inches are marked, as well as the tenths of inches. The basin of quicksilver is at the bottom.

THE SCIENCES

in the tube itself. The weight of the quicksilver in the tube pressing downward just balances the pressure of the air on the quicksilver in the basin. The two pressures just balance each other."

The Air Presses about Fifteen Pounds on Every Square Inch.—*Tom.* The height of the column of quicksilver in the tube is about thirty inches.

FIGURE 65

Fill (or partly fill) a tumbler with water and press a stout piece of writing paper over the top closely. Put the palm of your hand over the paper and hold it on tightly. Now quickly turn the tumbler upside down and take away your hand from the paper. (See the picture.) The pressure of the air *from below* is so much greater than the weight of the water, and of the small amount of air in the tumbler, that the paper will hold the water up. (This experiment should be tried in the schoolroom.)

Jack. Yes, and if the tube were an inch square, the column of quicksilver in it (thirty inches high and an inch square) would weigh fifteen pounds. The air pressure on the basin keeps that column standing. It keeps a weight of fifteen pounds standing.

Fred. That is what is meant by saying the air presses fifteen pounds on every square inch of your body, isn't it?

Jack. It presses fifteen square inches on every square inch of the whole world; on your body, on the ground, and on the water—everywhere. It presses down, and it presses up too.

Tom. How does it press up? I see that it presses down.

Fred. The air must press up, or the balloon would not rise.

Jack. That is one proof, and here is another that you can try for yourself. (See Figure 65)

How to Measure the Heights of Mountains.—"Now I want you to say what would happen if I had taken the barometer to the top of the mountain."

Mary. The air is lighter at the top of the mountain than it is here, and does not press down so much.

Tom. So the quicksilver in the tube would not stand so high; it would not have so much air pressure to balance.

Jack. Bravo! that is just right. At the level of the ocean all the air—the whole atmosphere—is above you, and it presses fifteen pounds on every square inch of the ground. The quicksilver stands thirty inches high. When you go up about 1000 feet the air above you presses less because

FIGURE 66 AN ANEROID BAROMETER (A BAROMETER WITHOUT QUICKSILVER)

Aneroid is a Greek word that means "without any liquid." Inside the outer metal case is a tightly sealed box containing no air. On this box the outside air presses, sometimes more, sometimes less. The little box changes its shape under this pressure, and things are so arranged that changes of pressure make a needle pointer move around a dial. This form of barometer is very convenient for travelers and seamen.

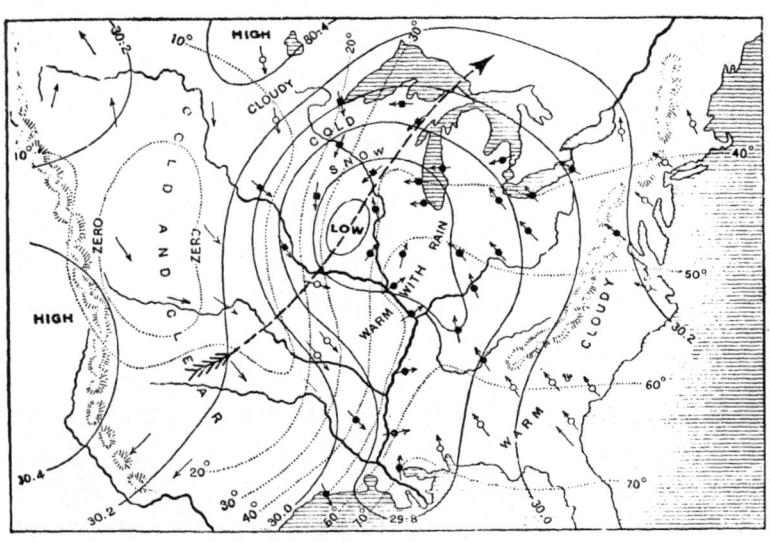

FIGURE 67

A map made by a Weather Bureau one November morning. An area of low barometer was near Omaha and it was moving towards Canada (in the direction of the curved arrow). Wherever there are little dots observations have been taken and telegraphed to Washington. The arrows through the dots fly with the wind—they point in the direction of the wind's motion at each place. Where the dots are black it was raining; where they are square it was snowing; where they are circles with white centers it was cloudy. The full lines (_____) join all places where the barometer was at the same height, as 30 4/10, 30 2/10, 30, 29 8/10 inches. The dotted lines (..........) join all the places where the thermometer stood the same, as 70 degrees, 60 degrees, 50 degrees, 40 degrees, 30 degrees, 20 degrees, 10 degrees, 0 degrees. There was zero weather near the Rocky Mountains, while it was warm and cloudy east of the Alleghenies. Northwest of the area of low barometer there was snow; southeast of it there was rain.

there is less of it; you have left 1000 feet of it below you, and the column of quicksilver is about twenty-nine inches high; if you go up 2000 feet, there is less air above you and the column is about twenty-eight inches high, and so on.

Tom. So you could measure the height of a mountain by noticing the height of the column of quicksilver in the tube? On high mountains the column would be short.

Jack. That is right, and that is the way the height of mountains are really measured. A barometer measures the weight of the air above you. The higher you go the less air above you and the less pressure on the basin of the barometer.

The Barometer is a Weatherglass.—*Fred.* Sometimes we see in the newspapers a notice of a storm. The Weather Bureau says there is an area of low barometer coming.

Jack. It happens that where storms are the air weighs less and the barometer is low—the column of quicksilver is short. In fine weather the air is heavy and presses down more; so the barometer is high and the column of quicksilver is long. If you watch the quicksilver from day to day, you will find this is the case, generally; when fine weather is coming or is here the barometer is high; when storms are coming or are here the barometer is low. So the barometer is a kind of weatherglass. It tells you beforehand what type of weather is coming.[1]

[1] Barometers often have words engraved opposite points of their scales; as: 30 ½ inches, *set fair* (meaning that the weather will be fair for some time); 30 inches, *fair;* 29 ½ inches, *change* (meaning expect a change soon); 29, *rain;*

THE SCIENCES

Fred. And it tells ships at sea when to look out for storms.

United States Weather Bureau Predictions.—*Jack.* Every day at a hundred places in the United States, in Cuba, and so forth, the observers of the Weather Bureau notice how their barometers are standing and telegraph to the central Weather Bureau at Washington. There they make a weather map of the whole country several times daily. If a storm is traveling eastwards, it will show on the map by an area of low barometer, as they call it. The barometer in the country round Omaha will be low on Monday, for instance; by Tuesday the storm has traveled to Buffalo; so the Weather Bureau tells New York to look out for a storm on Wednesday.

Agnes. Well, I never knew before how that was done.

Thermometers.[1]—*Fred.* A thermometer has quicksilver in it, too, but it is closed at both ends.

Tom. A thermometer is to measure how hot the air is. It is different from a barometer; that measures how heavy the air is.

Jack. Yes, a thermometer measures how hot the quicksilver in it happens to be by the height of the quicksilver in the glass tube. If the quicksilver column

---

28 ½, *much rain;* 28, *stormy.* The weather is foretold by a *change* in the barometer rather than by the actual height of the quicksilver. If the quicksilver is rising, then the weather is changing towards *fair;* if it is falling, then the weather is changing towards *stormy.*

[1] The word *thermometer* is from two Greek words, and it means "an instrument to measure heat—temperature."

PHYSICS

is long, then the temperature is high; if the column is short, then the temperature is low. The higher the temperature the longer is the quicksilver column.

Mary. It is like the iron tire of the cart wheel. (See Figure 55.) The hotter the fire, the longer the tire is.

Agnes. By just putting my hand on a thermometer I can make the quicksilver mount up in the tube.

Tom. Jack, why do they make the scale this way? 32° is marked freezing, and 212° is marked boiling.

Jack. A German named Fahrenheit[1] invented the thermometer we use about 200 years ago. (See the right-hand picture in Figure 68.) He put his thermometer into melting ice and made a mark on the tube just where the quicksilver stood; and then into boiling water and made a mark on the tube where the quicksilver stood. It is too complicated to tell you why he named the first mark 32° and the second 212°, but anyhow he did so. The distance between his two fixed marks is 180 equal parts—degrees. His thermometer was used in England; the Pilgrims

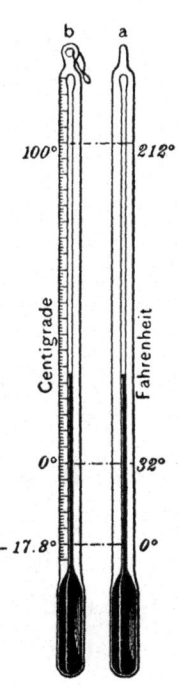

**FIGURE 68
THE GLASS
TUBES OF TWO
THERMOMETERS**

The tubes are closed at both ends are entirely empty of air, and are partly filled with quicksilver.

[1] Pronounced—far′en-hīt.

95

THE SCIENCES

brought it over to America; and we use it to-day. But there is another scale of degrees—the centigrade[1] (see the left hand picture in Figure 68)—which was invented in France about a hundred years ago, that is nearly everywhere in Europe. On the centigrade thermometer the freezing point is marked zero (0°), and the boiling point of water one hundred (100°); and the scale between 0 and 100 is divided into equal parts. Zero of Fahrenheit's scale is 17 8/10 degrees below the zero of centigrade scale. (See Figure 68.)

Mary. Was Centigrade a man?

Tom. Of course not; don't you see that *centi* means "one hundred," and *grade* means "degree"?

Mary. Why certainly; I thought he might be a Frenchman though.

Jack. If you put one of our thermometers into melting ice, it will always mark 32°; if you put it in boiling water, it will always mark 212°; and if you put the bulb of it in your mouth, it will always mark about 98°—that is, unless you have a fever.

Fred. The doctor always takes my temperature with a thermometer when I am ill.

Tom. And if your temperature goes as high as 104°, he looks very serious. The sign of being well is to have a temperature of 98°, they say.

Steam.—*Jack.* If you took a teakettle and boiled the water in it, the temperature of the boiling water would be 212°. Inside the kettle there is water at the bottom,

---

[1] Pronounced—sen′ti-grād

PHYSICS

and above the water there is steam. If we had a glass kettle, you could look through the sides and you would see nothing at all above the water. *True steam is invisible*; but there is steam there all the while. How do we know?

Fred. I thought steam was visible. What is that cloud coming out of the nozzle of the kettle?

Jack. That is water; cooled

Figure 69 A Teakettle with Boiling Water in it

It gives out clouds of what we call steam. The clouds are really not steam, but steam cooled back into water. If you hold an alcohol lamp under the cloud, the hot flame will turn it back into steam and you will se no cloud over the flame, because *true steam is invisible*. It is there though, as you can tell by holding a cold spoon over the invisible spot. The invisible steam will turn into visible water (like fog or cloud) and gather in drops on the spoon. (This experiment should be tried in the schoolroom.)

steam; water in small drops like fog or clouds. The real invisible steam is inside, trying to lift the lid and escape. If we fastened the lid down and closed the nozzle, we should have a little steam engine.

THE SCIENCES

The Steam Engine.—Then Jack explained the working of the steam engine to the children in this way. (See Figure 70.)

F is the firebox; *B* is the boiler with water in the bottom of it; *S* is the steam pipe that carries the live steam over to the valve chest *VC*. There are two pipes in the valve chest, pipe *M* and pipe *N*, and both pipes open from the valve chest and run to the cylinder *C*. But things are so arranged that *both pipes M and N cannot be open at the same time.* If *N* is open, *M* is shut (as in the picture). If *M* is open, *N* must be shut.

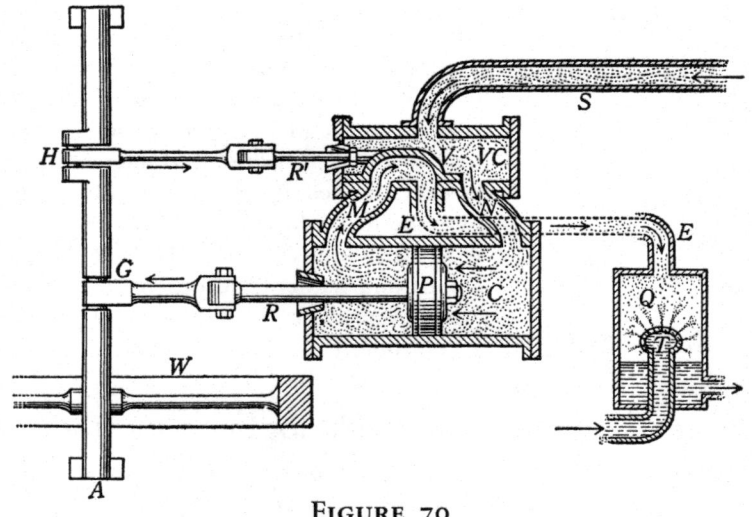

Figure 70
Drawing of part of a steam engine.

The picture is drawn with the pipe *N* open. The live steam rushes into the pipe *N*, fills it, and rushes into the right-hand end of the cylinder *C* and presses against the piston head *P*. (The piston head is a large iron disk that fills up the whole of the diameter of the cylinder.) The pressure of the live steam moves the piston head P (to the left in the picture) to the other end of the cylinder C and pushes the piston rod R against the crank G on the crank shaft A, and turns it. You must imagine now that the piston head P is at the left-hand end of the cylinder C and that the live steam fills the whole of the cylinder. Find the letter R' in the picture. R' is fastened to the slide valve V at one end and to the crank shaft at H, and things are so arranged that *now* the rod R' *closes* the pipe N by which the steam came in and at the same time *opens* the pipe M. The live steam is filling the valve chest VC all this time. It cannot get into the pipe N (which is now closed), and so it rushes into the pipe M (which is now open) and presses against the left-hand side of the piston head P (which is now at the left-hand end of the cylinder C). The piston is now pushed back by the steam to where it started from (just as in the picture), and the crank shaft A is turned still more. When the piston gets back to where it started the pipe M is closed and the pipe N is opened again (by the rod R') and the piston head is moved to the left again, then to the right, then to the left, and so on as long as the engine is running. Every time the piston head P travels the length of the cylinder C the crank G makes half a turn, and in this way the crank shaft GA keeps on turning. W' is a little pulley wheel fastened to the crank shaft; and if you put a leather belt on this pulley wheel, you can carry the power of the engine wherever you like. You can carry it as far as the belt goes and drive any other machine—a lathe, a saw, a drill. W is a heavy fly wheel fastened to the shaft A to keep the motion steady.

All this description of how an engine works is perfectly easy to understand if you take one thing at a time and pay attention; but it is rather long, and you had better read it over again carefully with a pin in your hand to point with. The live steam starts from the boiler *B* (put your pointer there); fills the valve chest *VC* (put your pointer there); rushes through the pipe *N* (point at it); presses against the piston head *P* (point at it); drives the piston head to the left-hand end of the cylinder (point at it); moves the stiff piston rod *R* so as to turn the crank *G* (point at *R* and *G*). At this time the pipe *N* is closed and the pipe *M* is open (point at *N* and *M*); the live steam is all the while filling the valve chest *VC* (point there) and cannot escape through the pipe *N* (which is closed) and now rushes through the pipe *M* (which is now open), and so on. You must go through the whole description again and again till you understand it.

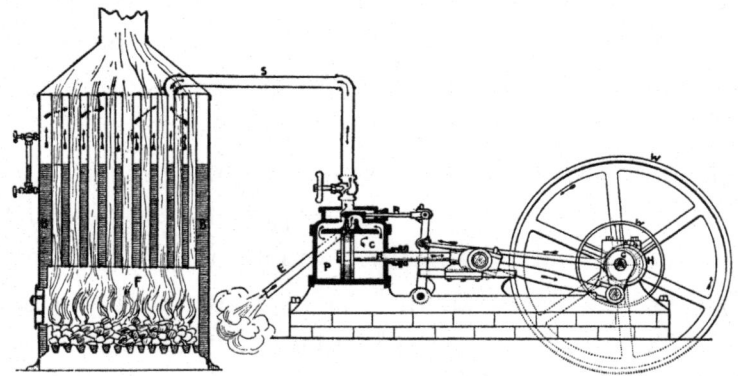

FIGURE 71 A STATIONARY STEAM ENGINE

C, cylinder; *P*, piston; *R*, piston rod. The reader should trace the course of the steam (which enters through the pipe *S*) throughout a complete motion of the piston.

The Locomotive.—Figures 70 and 71 show just how steam from a boiler can be made to turn a crank shaft (*G* in both pictures) round and round. Suppose we put wheels on this crank shaft and make the engine into a locomotive.

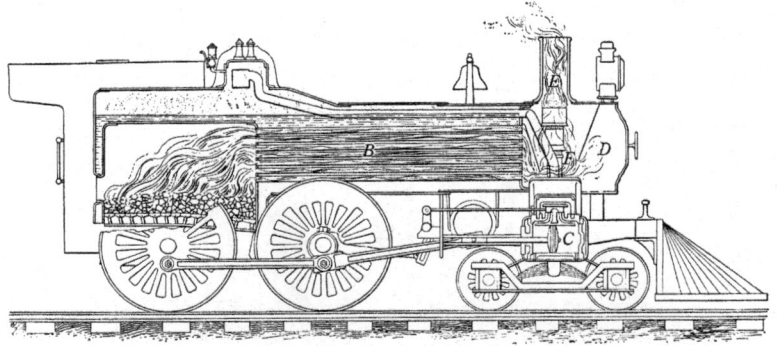

FIGURE 72 A LOCOMOTIVE ENGINE

A working engine removes steam very rapidly from the boiler. A railway locomotive consumes from 3 to 6 tons of water per hour. It is therefore necessary to have the fire in contact with as large a surface as possible. This end is accomplished in the tubular boiler by causing the flames to pass through a large number of metal tubes immersed in water. To suck the flames through the tubes *B* (Figure 72) of the boiler a powerful draft is required. This is obtained by running the exhaust steam from the cylinder *C* into the smokestack *E* through the blower *F*. The strong current through *F* draws with it a partial vacuum into which a powerful draft rushes from the furnace through the tubes *B*.

THE SCIENCES

The Gas Engine. The gas engine is also important. It is driven by properly timed explosions of a mixture of gas and air in the cylinder. It is free from smoke, very compact, and can be started at a moment's notice. It can do twice the work of the steam engine. The fuel (gas or gasoline) is fairly expensive. Most automobiles are run by gas engines. The light and efficient gas engine also made possible the airplane and the airship.

FIGURE 73   AN OCEAN STEAMSHIP

Light.—*Jack*. The very first thing to know about light is that it travels in straight lines. You cannot see round a corner, you know, though you can hear round a corner.

The room was darkened, and the sun's rays were let in through a very small hole in a card and made an oval spot on the floor. Tom took a newspaper, crumpled it up, and set it on fire in a coal hod, so that the room was partly filled with smoke and dust. This made it easy to trace each little sunbeam along its whole course, as the picture shows.

PHYSICS

FIGURE 74

The sun's rays travel in straight lines. (This experiment should be tried in the schoolroom.)

Fred. That spot on the floor looks like a picture of the sun.

Jack. It *is* a picture—an image—of the sun. It is oval because the sunlight falls slanting on the floor. But take this large sheet of white pasteboard and hold it perpendicular to the sun's rays and you will get a round image. You can get a picture of the landscape outside by letting light in through a small hole in the same way. (See Figure 75)

Mary. Well, I'm sure I don't understand how you can get a picture of out-of-doors by just letting light through a hole.

Jack. It is the easiest thing in the world to understand when it is explained; but it is not so easy to understand it when you see it the first time, as you have, Mary—when

THE SCIENCES

it is sprung on you, as the boys say.

Fred. Well, Jack, how is it? Explain it to us, now that you have sprung it on us.

Jack. It all comes from light traveling in straight lines. Let us begin with a simple case, and explain the harder one afterwards.

FIGURE 75 A PICTURE OF THE LANDSCAPE FORMED INSIDE A DARK ROOM (*Camera obscura*) BY LIGHT THAT PASSES THROUGH A VERY SMALL HOLE

This experiment can be tried in the schoolroom. The room should be quite dark. The hole should be pierced in a sheet of cardboard or, better, a neat hole should be drilled in a sheet of tin.

The light of the candle (Figure 76) travels in straight lines. So does the light from every brilliant thing. Every point of the sun and every part of a candle flame is always sending out rays of light, and the rays go off in every possible direction.

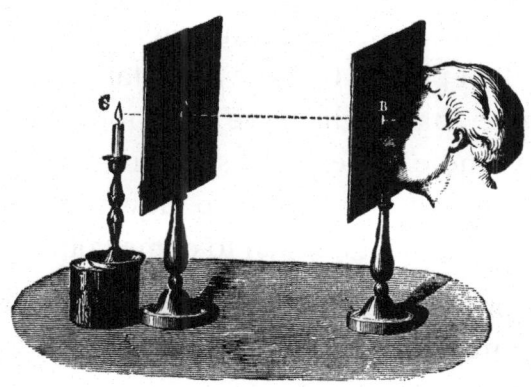

Figure 76

The light of a candle travels in straight lines. Until you have the candle (*C*) and the two holes (*A* and *B*) in the same straight line you cannot see the flame. (This experiment should be tried in the schoolroom.)

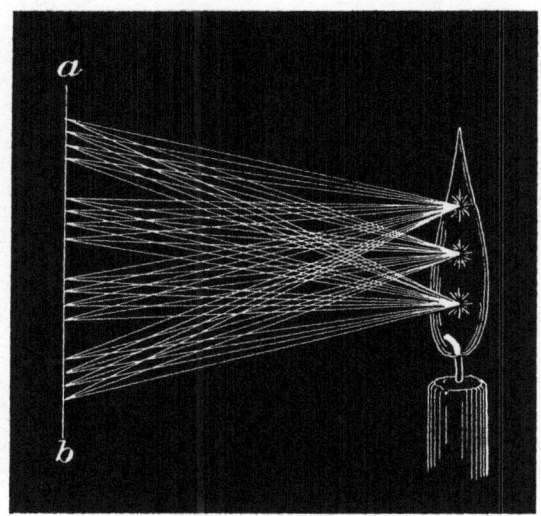

Figure 77

Some of the rays from three points of a candle flame are drawn in this picture. They fall on a screen (*ab*) and make it bright. From every point of the flame there are such rays. And there are many more than are drawn in the picture.

THE SCIENCES

If you take a pincushion shaped like a ball and stick it full of pins so that the pins stand out all over it everywhere, that might serve as a model of a brilliant point of a candle flame. Every such point sends out rays of light in every direction—up, down, sidewise. You "see" by the rays that happen to come your way.

Rays of light from the candle flame go out in every possible direction. How do you know that, Tom?

Tom. Because you can see the candle flame no matter what part of the room you are in. If you see it, you must get rays from it.

Figure 78
In a dark room a candle shining through a pin hole will form its own image on a screen.

Jack. Exactly; now most of the rays from the flame light up the card and the table and the walls of the

PHYSICS

room; a few of them—only a few—get through the hole in the card (Figure 78). Some ray from the top of the flame gets to the hole, goes through it, and goes on till it meets the screen of white pasteboard. There it stops, and there you have an image of the top of the flame. Some ray from the candle wick gets through the hole and goes on to meet the screen and, when it meets it, forms an image of the wick. Some rays from each of the other parts of the flame get through the hole and make images, so that finally an image of the whole flame is shown on the screen. The image of the flame is built up of hundreds of little separate images, you see.[1]

Agnes. The image of the candle on the screen is upside down, and so was the picture of the landscape (Figures 75 and 78).

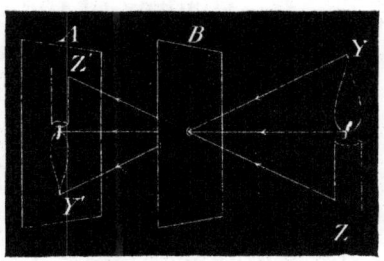

FIGURE 79
The image of candle shining through a pin hole is formed upside down on a screen, and this drawing shows why.

---

[1] The reader should lay a straight edge (the edge of a card will do) on Figure 78. He will see that the wick, the hole, and the image of the wick are in one straight line. Again, the top of the flame, the hole, and the image of the top of the flame are in one straight line, and so on.

THE SCIENCES

Jack. You can see why it was so from this drawing, Agnes.

Shadows.—"The shadow of any square or cube is bounded by straight lines (Figure 78), and this is another proof that light travels in straight lines. When the point of light is really a point, or when it is only a small spot (as in the electric street lamp) the edges of the shadow are sharp; but when the light comes from a large body like the sun the true shadow (the *umbra*) is bordered by a less dark shadow (the *penumbra*). If you hold a piece of cardboard in front of a lighted candle in a dark room, you can see the shadow of the cardboard on the wall. The shadow is made up of two parts—the dark center (the *umbra*) and a less dark part (the *penumbra*). Move the cardboard till it is quite near the wall and you will see the *umbra* get dark and sharp and the *penumbra* almost disappear."[1]

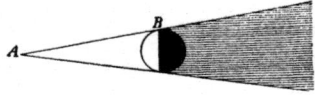

FIGURE 80

A point of light at *A* lights half of a globe at *B*, and *B* casts a shadow. The electric street lamp casts a shadow with sharp edges as in the picture, because the light of an electric street lamp comes from a very small spot—a point of light.

Eclipses of the Sun and Moon.—Eclipses of the sun and moon can be explained by Figure 81. The globe of the lamp stands for the sun, the ball *B* for the earth, the ball *C* for the moon.

---

[1] This experiment should be tried in the darkened schoolroom. When the appearances are thoroughly understood a second candle should be lighted and the shadows of the two made to overlap.

PHYSICS

Suppose you were on the earth (*B*) inside the shadow of the moon. (Take a pin and point out the place.) The sun would be hidden from you if you were there; the sun would be eclipsed to you. *An eclipse of the sun occurs for any place on the earth when that place is in the moon's shadow.* (See Figure 51.)

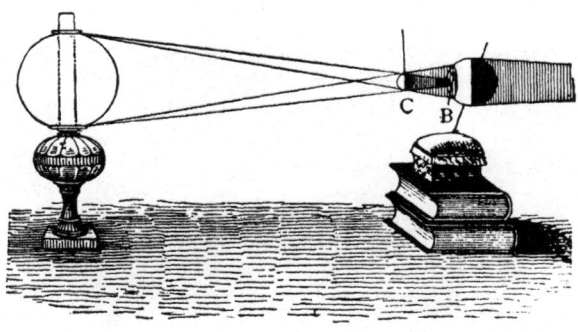

FIGURE 81

A schoolroom experiment on shadows. The room must be dark and the lamp should have a ground-glass globe. The ball *B* may be an orange fastened to the pincushion by a knitting needle. The little ball *C* (a small ball of twine) can be suspended by a string so as to cast a shadow on the globe *B*. Notice that the ball *C* has two shadows, a dark central shadow (the *umbra*) and a less dark shadow around it (the *penumbra*). The *large* brilliant globe of the lamp makes two shadows to *C*. (By a little thinking you can see why.)

The moon revolves around the earth, you know. Take the little ball *C* and suspend it on that side of the ball B which is farthest from the lamp. It will be in the shadow of the ball *B*. When the moon is in the shadow of the earth no light from the sun can reach it, and it is eclipsed. *An eclipse of the moon occurs whenever the moon is in the shadow of the earth.*

THE SCIENCES

Reflection of Light.—*Jack.* Light that falls on any surface is reflected from it. That is the way we see the surface. The sunlight falls on the ground and is reflected up to our eyes, else we should not see the ground. A feather that is floating in the air reflects light to us, else we should not see it. The moon floating in the sky reflects the sunlight to us, else we should not see it.

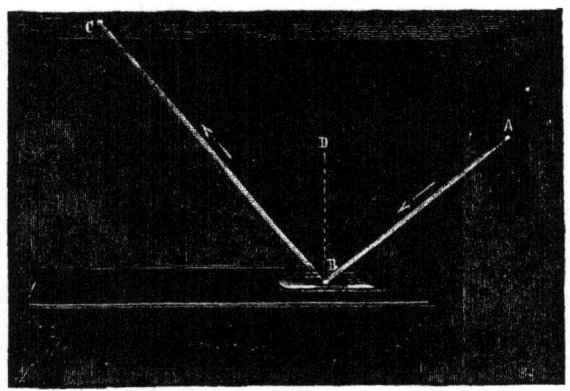

FIGURE 82

A beam of light enters a dark room through a hole in the wall (A) and falls on a mirror at B. It is reflected from the mirror upwards to form a spot on the ceiling at C. By putting a pencil vertically at B, in the line BD, you will see that the ray of light AB and the ray of light BC make the same angles with the pencil BD. That is, the angles ABD and CBD are always equal to each other, no matter where the mirror may be.

Fred. The sun sends us its own light though. We do not see it by reflected light.

Jack. The sun, the stars, an electric lamp, a candle, have light of their own. They send us light directly. The moon, the planets, distant mountains and clouds, nearby houses and rocks and fields, reflect sunlight to us. If you could shut off the sunlight, you would not see them.

PHYSICS

Tom. The sunlight *is* shut off at night (at least it is shut off from everything on the earth) and you do not see the mountains and the houses then.[1]

Refraction of Light.—*Jack.* Light always travels in straight lines; but when a ray of light that has been traveling along one straight line in the air enters something different from air—water or glass, for instance—it is bent (refracted) into another line. This second line is straight, too; but it is not the same line as the first one.

Water will bend a ray of light, and so will glass. You know what a prism is? A glass pendant to a chandelier is a prism, for instance.

If you let sunlight pass through a prism and then fall on a sheet of paper, you will get a beautiful *spectrum* of all the colors of the rainbow. If a plate of glass or a metal mirror is ruled with fine parallel lines equally distant, say 1000 or 10,000 to the inch, you can get a beautiful spectrum

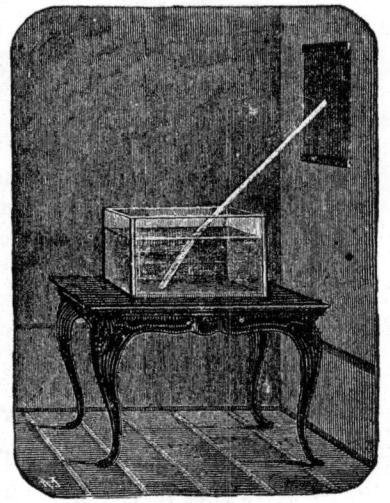

FIGURE 83

A ray of sunlight enters a dark room through a hole in the wall, and it falls on water contained in a box with glass sides (a box with one glass side will do). The ray is bent (refracted) as soon as it enters the water.

---

[1] The reasons why you see the moon and the planets at night are explained in Astronomy, page 35.

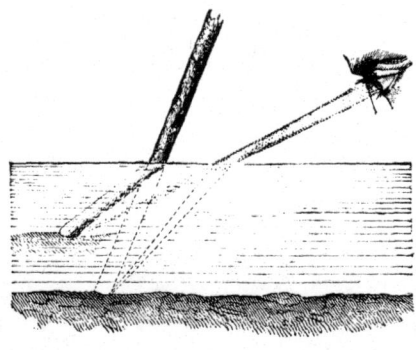

FIGURE 84

A straight stick partly out of the water and partly in the water *looks* as if it were bent just where it enters the water. Of course it is not really bent, but it looks so. Try the experiment with a pencil in a shallow basin full of water.

by laying it out in the sunshine. The colors of mother-of-pearl are made in this way. The inside of the oyster shell is made up of very fine parallel ridges, and the light reflected from them is scattered into a spectrum of colors. You can prove that it is the ridges that make the colors by taking an impression of the inside of the mother-of-pearl shell in wax. The wax gives just the same colors. The scattering of sunlight by raindrops in somewhat the same way has to do with forming the rainbow.

Lenses.—"Pieces of glass or certain shapes are called *lenses*. We use them to make magnifying glasses, spectacles, microscopes, telescopes. You children had better get some old spectacle glasses and try experiments with them. (See Figures 45, 88-90)

"Two (or more) lenses used together make a telescope, you know.[1] Convex lenses concentrate the light that falls on them (Figure 89), and concave lenses disperse the light that falls on them. Persons who are nearsighted use concave lenses in their spectacles, and persons who are farsighted use convex lenses."

[1] See Astronomy, page 62.

FIGURE 85

A glass prism is mounted, for convenience, on a stand; but the experiment can be tried by a prism held in the hand. The candle flame seen through the prism seems to be in a different place from the real candle flame, because the rays of light sent out by the flame are bent by the prism and when they come to the eye they seem to come from a place where the real candle is not.

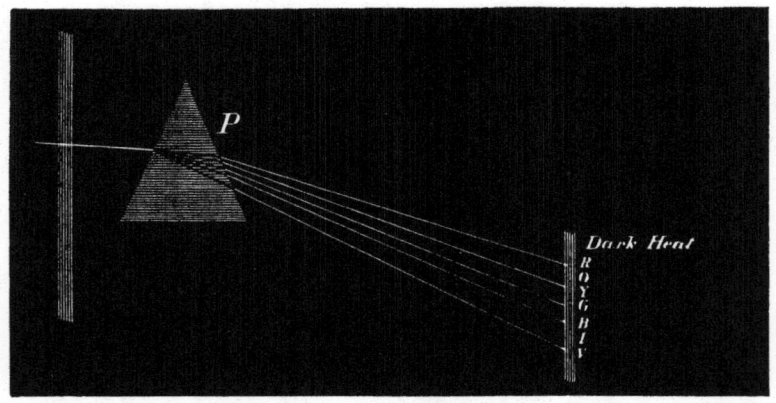

FIGURE 86

A beam of sunlight (white light) is separated by a prism into rays of violet, indigo, blue, green, yellow, orange, and red, and most of the heat in the beam falls near the red end of the spectrum. The heat rays are invisible.

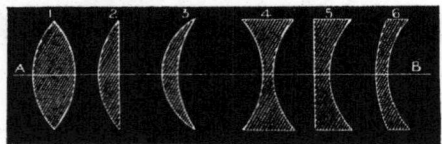

FIGURE 87 GLASS LENSE OF DIFFERENT SHAPES

The three to the left of the middle of the picture are convex lenses; the other three are concave lenses.

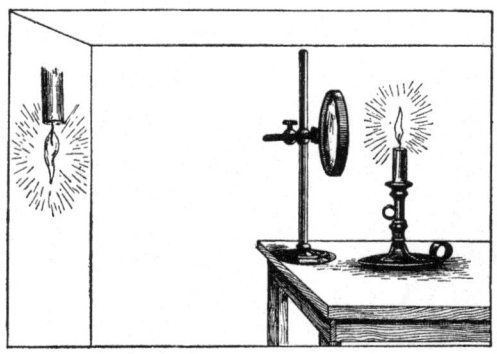

FIGURE 88

A convex lens in a dark room will make a sharp image of a candle flame on the wall if the lens is at the right distance. (The distance to the wall must be different for different lenses and can be found by trial.)

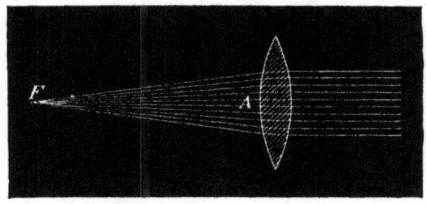

FIGURE 89

A convex lens concentrates light falling on it to a focus (at F in the picture.)

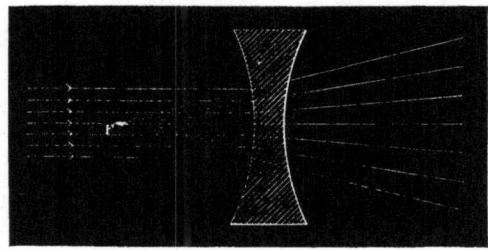

FIGURE 90

A concave lens disperses light falling on it. (The light comes from F in the picture and is dispersed by the lens.)

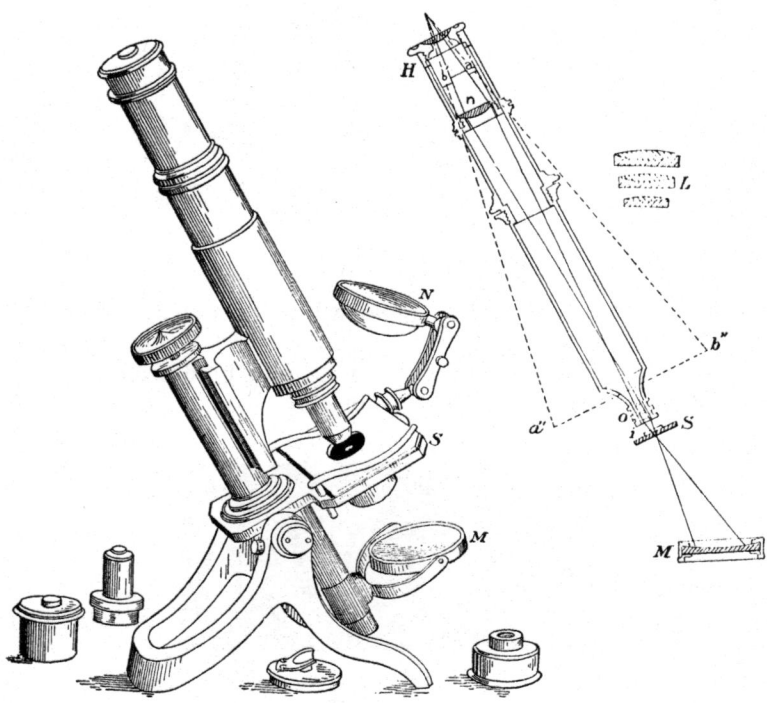

FIGURE 91   A POWERFUL MICROSCOPE

The object to be examined is placed on the stand S and looked at through the long tube. Light can be thrown on the object by the lens N or by the mirror M. The right-hand picture shows the way the lenses are arranged in the tube. The eye is placed near H, and there is one lens there, another at n, and three others at O (an enlarged picture of these three is given at L). Such a microscope as this can be arranged so as to magnify about 2000 times—to make things seem 2000 times larger.

PHYSICS

Velocity of Sound and Light.—The children were sitting on the porch one afternoon when they heard the church bell in the village ringing.

Agnes. Listen to the bell! how plainly you can hear it, and yet it is nearly three miles away.

Mary. Two—three—four. It is four o'clock. The hammer has just this moment struck the bell.

Fred. You mean the hammer struck the bell a moment ago, and we have heard it this minute.

Mary. Why do you say that, Fred?

Fred. You know that you do not hear the sound of a blow when the blow is struck—not till afterwards. Haven't you ever seen a gun fired by a man a mile away from you and then waited to hear the sound?

Mary. Why do you have to wait?

Fred. Why, you know the light of the flash comes to you instantly—the very minute the gun is fired; and it takes time for the sound to travel. Let us ask Jack to tell us how fast sound travels; he is sure to know.

Jack. Light travels almost infinitely fast;[1] but sound moves much slower—about 1100 feet in a second. It takes sound nearly five seconds to go a mile.

Mary. Do you mean, Jack, that we didn't hear the village clock strike till fifteen seconds after it had really struck?

[1] The velocity of light is 186,330 miles in a *second* of time. Light travels from the sun to the earth in 500 seconds, a little more than eight minutes

Jack. Yes; the hammer struck the bell first and set it vibrating; then the air round the bell began to vibrate, and the sound began to travel off in every direction— north, east, south, west. If you had been in the village, you would have heard the bell the moment it was struck; if you had been a mile away, you would have heard it five seconds late; and as we are three miles away, we all heard it about fifteen seconds later.

FIGURE 92 A CHURCH BELL

It is rung by the rope that you see on the left-hand side of the picture.

PHYSICS

Tom. It is something like throwing a stone into a pond of water. Little waves travel in every direction from the place where the stone went into the pond.

FIGURE 93

A wave of sound if it were visible, as it is not, would look something like the picture. Such waves go out from a sounding bell in every direction. When they come to your ear you hear the bell, but not before. Sound waves travel about 1100 feet in a second—a mile in about five seconds.

Jack. Yes; and you remember that the waves get smaller and smaller the farther they go. Sound is like that. The vibrations of the air are powerful near the sounding bell, but they get weaker and weaker as you go away from it.

Tom. So sound is a vibration is it, Jack?

Jack. There would be no sound unless there were some vibration in the first place. But there wouldn't be any *sound* unless there were some person to hear it. If there were a mechanical piano playing at the north pole, by machinery, there would be vibration of the strings—and of the air, too; but unless there were some one to hear it there would be no sound, only vibration.

Tom. Well, usually there are persons to hear in our part of the world. Are all the sounds we hear caused by vibrations?

Musical Instruments.—*Jack.* Yes; let us take some sounds we know about and see what makes them. In the first place there is the bell. The hammer strikes it and makes it vibrate. It is just the same with a piano;

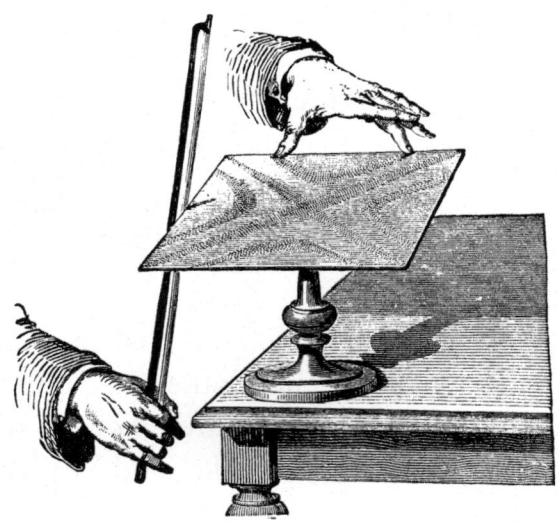

FIGURE 94

A glass plate vibrates when a fiddle bow is drawn across its edge so that the plate makes a sound. If you put a little clean dry sand on the plate, the sand will move so as to make patterns (as in the cut). By drawing the bow at different places you can get different patterns, especially if you lightly touch the plate with a lead pencil while the bow is moving. Some of the patterns are shown in the next picture.

the wire is struck and made to vibrate. A violin string vibrates. In an organ pipe or in a trumpet the air vibrates. When you speak or sing a couple of elastic muscles in your throat vibrate. In a drum the parchment vibrates when the drumsticks strike. Something always vibrates first; that, whatever it is, sets the air to vibrating, and the vibration travels to where we happen to be and we hear a sound.

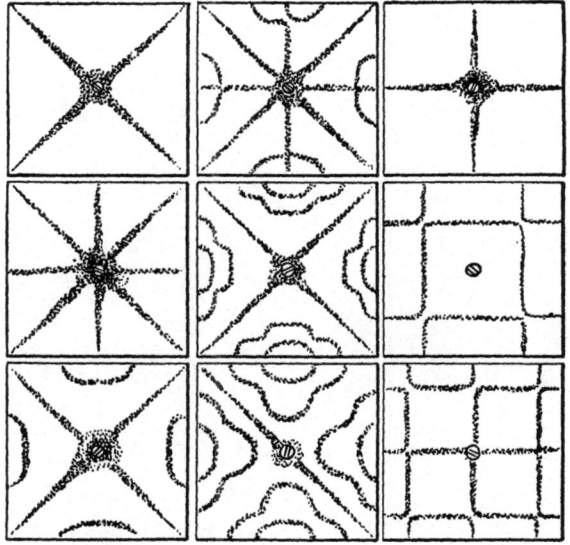

FIGURE 95 PATTERNS MADE BY LOOSE SAND ON A VIBRATING PLATE (SEE FIGURE 94)

After the patterns have been made they can be preserved by carefully pouring varnish on the plate and letting it dry.

Tom. How do you know that the bell vibrates?

Jack. The next time you are in the village go up in the clock tower when the clock is going to strike and hold a lead pencil against the bell. You can *feel* the bell vibrate.

THE SCIENCES

Here is a curious thing to think of. First the bell vibrates and you can hear it for miles in every direction. Every particle in a very large sphere of air is set in motion. We hear the sound at our house, miles away from the village. Now the air that is set in motion weighs hundreds of tons, and it is all moved by one stroke of the hammer on the bell.

Tom. You can hear a locust chirping a quarter of a mile off. I suppose he sets the whole air in motion, too.

FIGURE 96

A watch ticking in front of one mirror can be plainly heard through a tube placed in front of another. If you take the second mirror away, you cannot hear it at all. The first mirror acts as a speaking trumpet (a *megaphone*), and the second mirror acts as an ear trumpet.

PHYSICS

Jack. That is a very good example. A small insect moves tons and tons of air; and a violin string, vibrating so little that you can hardly see it move, stirs all the air in a great concert hall.

Sometimes when the organ is playing a low note in church you can actually hear the air flutter and vibrate. The organ makes a noise then, not music.

Mary. What is the difference between noise and music, Jack?

Jack. If the vibrations of a bell, a violin string, an organ pipe—anything—come at even intervals, then they make a musical note. If they come irregularly, the sound is usually a mere noise. Music is pleasant to hear, and noise is not. That is the real difference.

Reflection of Sound.—Sound can be reflected somewhat as light is, as the following experiment shows.

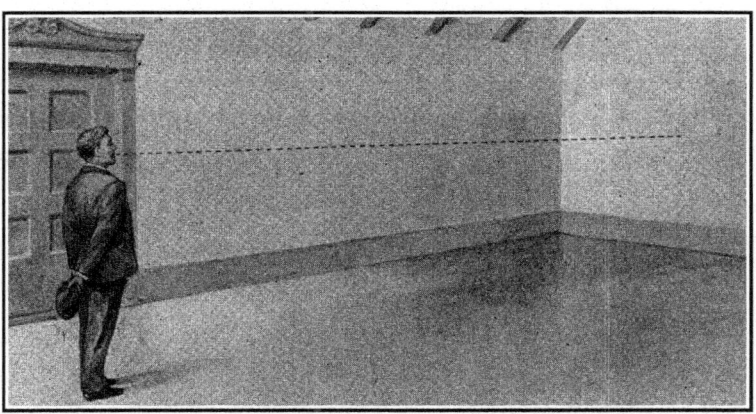

FIGURE 97   ECHOES

An echo is made by the reflection of sound from a wall, a rock, etc. The person who speaks must be at least 100 feet away from the wall to get a good echo.

THE SCIENCES

Musical Notes.—*Mary*. Are the sounds from my piano regular?

Jack. Yes; perfectly regular. Each string vibrates regularly just so many times in a second, no more and no less. The middle C of your piano is a wire just long enough to vibrate 261 times every second, and all of its vibrations are alike.

The shorter a string is the quicker it vibrates, and you will notice that the highest notes of your piano come from the shortest strings. It is the same with drums; the small drums give the highest notes, the large drums the lowest.

The Voice.— *Tom*. But what sets the air into vibration to make the sounds when we talk?

Fred. The sounds come from our Adam's apples, don't they?

Jack. Yes, and the proper name for the Adam's apple is the larynx. It is located at the upper end of the windpipe. In it are two flat stretched bands that project into the opening somewhat like shelves (Figure 99). These bands lie far apart and are not stretched when we are not speaking, but as soon as we begin to talk, the bands are brought close together and are stretched. Air is forced out of the lungs past their edges, so setting them into vibration and producing sound. These bands are called vocal cords, although they do not look very much like

FIGURE 98 TRACE MADE BY A VIBRATING FORK

cords. The sounds that they make are modified by the shape and size of the throat, mouth, nasal chambers, and other features which you can think of for yourselves.

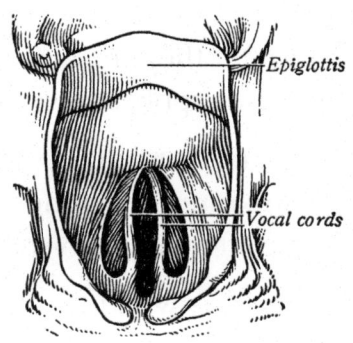

FIGURE 99
THE VOCAL CORDS

The Phonograph.— *Jack.* The phonograph is a machine for recording the vibrations of the air that are made when a person speaks. He speaks into a tube and sets the air into vibration. At the small end of the tube is a little round thin metal plate called a diaphragm that moves up and down (slightly) as the air vibrates. The motions of this little plate copy the vibrations of the air. On the lower side of this thin plate is a sharp needle point. The point of the needle is in contact with a smooth wax surface which is moved under the point as a disk record is moved in the phonograph. The needle cuts a groove in the wax. If the diaphragm vibrates, moving the needle up and down, the depth of the groove varies in accordance with the vibrations. In some types of instruments the needle moves sideways instead of up and down. The soft records are copied in harder materials for sale as the familiar phonograph records.

Tom. If the phonograph had been invented in Julius Cæsar's time, we might be able to hear his voice now, or George Washington's, or Lincoln's.

Jack. The records of the speeches of some of the

great men of to-day actually have been preserved; and long after they are dead, other people will know exactly how they spoke.

Mary. It would be a find thing for us to get Eleanor to sing into the phonograph now, so that when we go home after vacation we could still hear her!

Jack. A wise man in England[1] once suggested that there could be no worse punishment in a future life than to be forced perpetually to hear all the foolish things you had said in this life. It might not be a bad way to punish naughty boys and girls in *this* world to shut them up in a room with phonographs that would continually repeat the silly and foolish things they had said.

Agnes. I think it would be dreadful, Jack. Nothing could be worse.

Jack. Very well, my dear, *you* need not mind. The things you say are always nice to hear. I was only trying to frighten the boys.

Electricity. The children made some experiments in electricity which any one of you can make too, if you like. You will need a few things, most of which you can get at home or make for yourself. A few you will have to buy (they do not cost much). The principal things to get are: a couple of toy magnets, one straight, one shaped like a horseshoe; a piece of glass tube (or a glass rod) about half an inch in diameter and eight or ten inches long; a piece of sealing wax about half an inch square and about six inches long; a rubber comb; an

[1] Charles Babbage (born 1792, died 1871).

old silk handkerchief; a piece of old flannel; an ounce of sulphuric acid in a bottle with a glass stopper (be careful not to get the acid on your hands, and be sure that the bottle is labeled *Sulphuric Acid*); an ounce of quicksilver in a bottle (be sure that the quicksilver is labeled; it is poisonous if swallowed); about twenty feet or so of insulated copper wire (No. 18 annunciator wire is the most handy to use); a piece of sheet copper about three sixteenths of an inch thick, one and one half

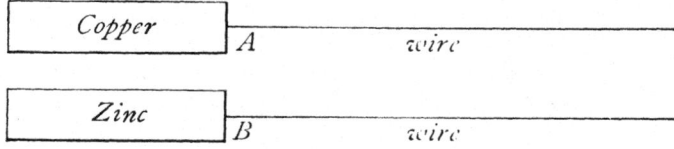

FIGURE 100

inches wide, and five inches long; a piece of sheet zinc of the same size as the copper. Take the copper sheet and the zinc sheet to a plumber and have him solder a piece of copper wire (each piece about twelve inches long) at *A* and *B*. After this is done take a large tumbler, fill it two-thirds full of water, pour three tablespoonfuls of sulphuric acid in it (use an old kitchen spoon for this purpose), dip the zinc plate in it, and leave it there for a minute. Then take the zinc plate out, hold it over a china plate, pour quicksilver on it, and rub the quicksilver on to the surface of the zinc until it is all covered and shining. (Do not empty the water and acid from the tumbler; you will need it by and by; save it.) Now you have all the things you need for your experiments, but

THE SCIENCES

it is *convenient* to get two *double connectors* (so called) like Figure 101.

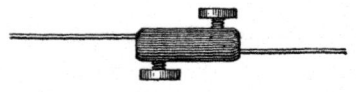

FIGURE 101

A double connector (so called) is a cylinder of brass with two holes in it and with two screws. It is used to connect the ends of two wires and saves the trouble of twisting the ends together. It is convenient, though not necessary.

Jack. Before we begin our experiments with the things you have collected, tell me what you already know about electricity. You have heard it talked about. Tell me what you have seen on your own account.

Agnes. Well, lightning is electricity, they say.

Mary. And electric bells ring by electricity, and some street railways go by electricity.

Fred. And then there is the electric telegraph.

Tom. Yes, and the telephone, and the electric light.

Jack. All these things have to do with electricity. Let us begin by making some lightning.

Agnes. Oh, Jack! make lightning? It would be dangerous.

Tom. Agnes thinks Jack can make anything—even a thunderstorm if he wants to.

Jack. Well, Agnes, the lightning we are going to make will not be dangerous; but I will put off making it for a little while and begin with something else.

Here is a lot of small pieces of tissue paper—they are very light, you see—laid on the table. Now take the glass rod, Agnes, and hold it over them. What happens?

PHYSICS

Agnes. Nothing happens at all.

Jack. Try the rubber comb, Mary.

Mary. Well, nothing happens.

Jack. Now, Agnes, rub the glass rod briskly with the silk handkerchief; and you, Mary, rub the comb with the flannel; and try again; Agnes first.

Agnes. Why, Jack! the little pieces of paper rise up to meet the glass. (See Figure 102)

FIGURE 102

Little pieces of tissue paper (or light grains of sawdust) are attracted by a glass rod rubbed with a silk handkerchief (or by a piece of sealing wax or a rubber comb rubbed with flannel).

Jack. Take the glass rod away, Agnes; and now, Mary try with your comb.

Mary. It is just the same thing; the little pieces of paper rise up to meet the comb—it is like magic.

Jack. We have learned something, anyway. What have we learned, Fred, so far?

THE SCIENCES

Fred. We have learned that if you rub a glass rod with silk, the rod will attract pieces of paper as a magnet attracts pieces of iron.

Tom. And that if you rub a piece of rubber[1] with flannel, the same thing happens.

Jack. That is very good so far. Now, Agnes, rub the glass rod with the flannel, not the silk; and Mary, rub the comb[2] with the silk, and both of you try once more. What happens?

Agnes. Nothing happens now.

Mary. Nothing happens when I try with the comb either.

Jack. Well, we have learned that to lift the little pieces of paper with a glass rod you must rub the rod with silk, not flannel; and the comb with flannel, not silk. Glass rubbed with silk is made electric—electrified, as they call it; and rubber (or sealing wax) rubbed with flannel is electrified. When either glass or rubber is so electrified it will attract little pieces of paper, or light grains of sawdust.

I want you all to try this experiment, too. Electrify the glass rod and the comb and then hold them near your face. What happens?

Agnes. Why it tickles! it feels as if there were a cobweb on my cheek.

---

[1] A piece of sealing wax rubbed with flannel will act just as the rubber comb acts. Try it.

[2] A piece of amber does the same thing. The Greek name for amber is elektron, and we get the name "electricity" that way.

PHYSICS

Jack. Tom, take the glass rod and rub it smartly with the silk. Now hold your knuckle close down to the tube. See there is a little spark.

Tom. I felt it and I heard it, too.

Jack. Agnes, that spark was lightning and the crackling noise was thunder, only they are not dangerous. Real lightning is just the same kind of thing as that little spark, and real thunder is just like the little noise that spark made. Perhaps you know that in 1752 Benjamin Franklin sent a kite up in the air during a thunderstorm and brought down some of the electricity that was in the clouds and proved that the lightning in the sky was exactly the same thing as the spark you have just seen.

FIGURE 103 A LONG ELECTRIC SPARK BETWEEN
TWO ELECTRIFIED BALLS

Lightning takes the shape of this spark. It is never a zigzag bolt made up of straight lines, as it often seems to be.

Now you children have seen the kind of electricity that makes thunder and lightning. Let us make some of the kind that they use in the telegraph. I want to make a current of electricity that I can use to carry a message from New York to San Francisco.

Now we shall need our tumbler of water with the

acid in it and the strips of copper and zinc. (See page 127.) Stand the two strips upright in the tumbler and put some strips of wood across the top of the tumbler to keep the zinc and copper apart. They must not touch anywhere. When you have arranged this all right so that everything will stay in place you have got a battery, and if you join the two wires (see the picture, Figure 104) a current of the electricity will flow from the copper plate to the zinc. I am going to prove it to you.

Take the end of the wire from the copper and put it on one side of your tongue and put the wire from the zinc on the other side, and you'll feel a little current passing. The current goes from the copper through the wire, and through your tongue to the zinc. Your tongue connects the two wires. If you actually join the two wires, the current will be there just the same. Feeling it with your tongue proves that it is there, and that is what I wanted to prove. If you had two such batteries joined together, you would have a current twice as strong. With many

FIGURE 104

A glass jar containing dilute sulphuric acid with a plate of zinc and a plate of copper in it (they must not touch each other) is called an *electric battery*. If you join the copper *(C)* and the zinc *(Z)* plates by a wire *(M)*, a current of electricity will flow from C to Z through the wire; no matter how long the wire is, the current will still flow. It would flow (with a strong current) from New York to Boston.

PHYSICS

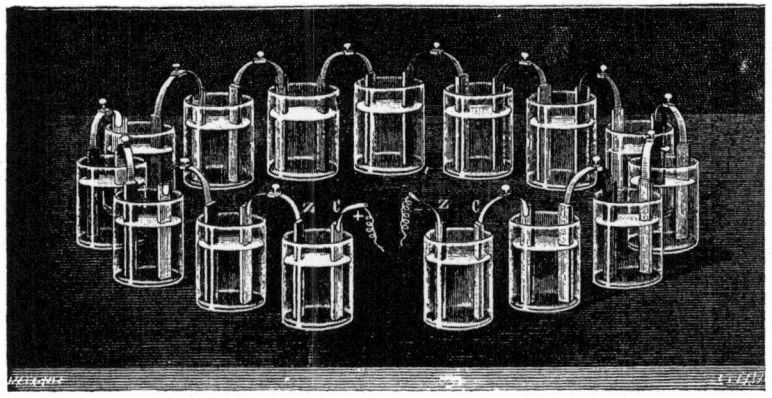

FIGURE 105   A BATTERY OF FIFTEEN CUPS
Notice that the zinc of one cup is connected to the copper of the next one, and so on. At the ends there are two short wires marked + and —. If you join these to two telegraph wires reaching a distant town, a current of electricity will flow from + to the distant town and back from the town to —. There would be a continuous circuit of wire from + to the town, and back again to —. If you cut the circuit of wire anywhere and put the two ends of the wire to your tongue, you will feel the current. That is proof that the current is always there, in the wire. It is always flowing so long as the battery is joined to the long loop, or circuit of wire.

batteries joined together,[1] you would have a current strong enough to travel over a wire as long as from New York to Boston; and that is the kind of electricity they use in telegraphing.

The Telegraph.—"I understand how you send a current of electricity from New York to Boston," said Tom; "you have a battery at New York and a loop of wire—what you call a circuit—going to Boston and returning to New York, this way:

---

[1] The zinc of one battery to the copper of the next one.

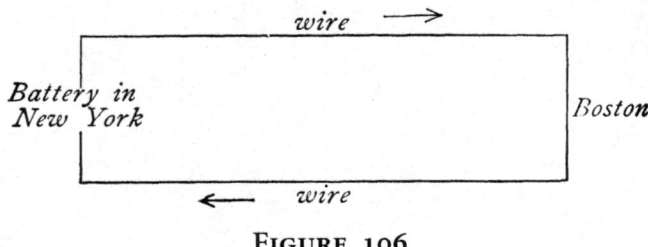

FIGURE 106

But I don't see how you make the signals. The current flows through the wires quietly; it makes no noise."

Fred. You have to put telegraph instruments—a key and so forth—on the wire, don't you?

Jack. Yes; we can improve Tom's drawing by putting them in, this way:

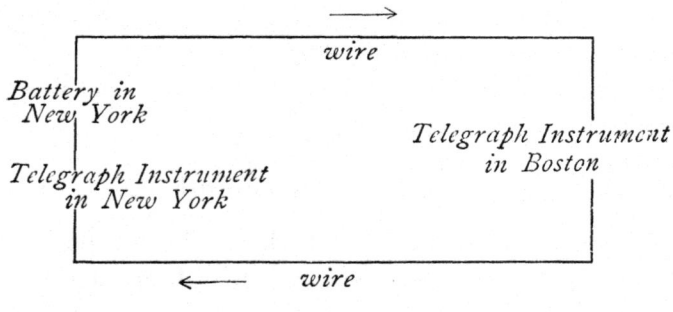

FIGURE 107

The battery in New York is all the while sending a current of electricity along the wire. It fills the whole of the wire from New York to Boston and back again. It flows along the wire and through the telegraph instruments at both places. When you wish to talk to Boston you move your New York key up and down, and the receiving instrument in Boston makes little sounds,

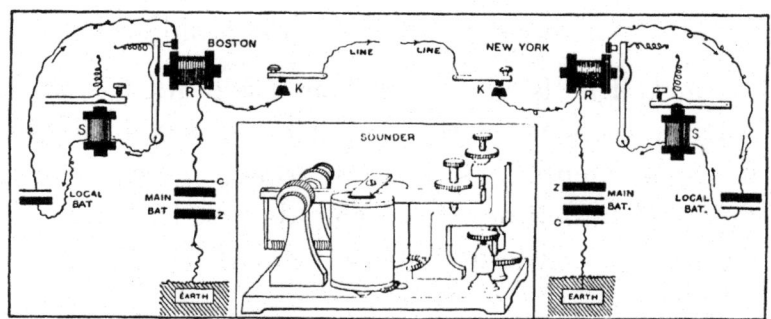

FIGURE 108

This figure shows the way in which New York and Boston are connected by telegraph. It is more complicated than the way described before, but the idea is the same. The key at New York is marked K (the K on the right-hand side). If this key is tapped, a signal goes over the wire to Boston and is received on a sounder there. (See the picture of the sounder at the bottom of the cut.) In the same way signals made with the Boston key are heard on the New York sounder.

THE SCIENCES

one sound for each motion of the New York key. You can arrange an alphabet that way. For instance, three dots (. . .) might be C, one dot (.) might be E, and two dots (. .) might be I. You could spell *ice*, for example, this way: [.., ..., .].

Fred. And Boston could talk to New York by dotting with the Boston key, and New York would hear it.

Jack. That is exactly the way it is done. Go into a telegraph office sometime and listen, and you will hear the instruments clicking away. Sometimes they make dots and sometimes larger sounds called dashes, and sometimes very long dashes. The alphabet they use is:

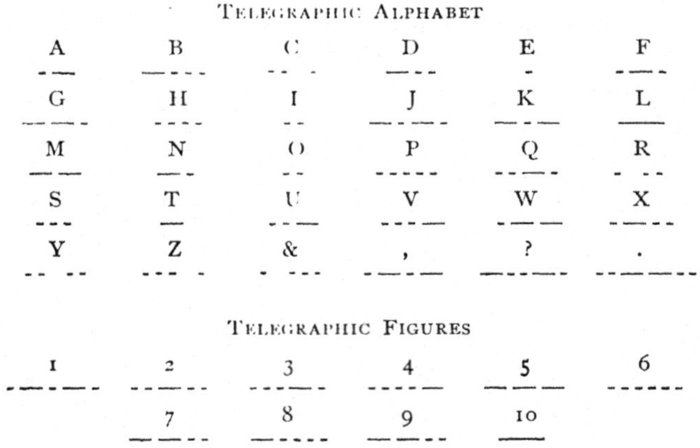

TELEGRAPHIC ALPHABET

A	B	C	D	E	F
.—	—...	.. .	—..	.	..—.
G	H	I	J	K	L
——.	....	..	—.—.	—.—	——
M	N	O	P	Q	R
——	—.	. .	.....	..—.	. ..
S	T	U	V	W	X
...	—	..—	...—	.——	.—..
Y	Z	&	,	?	.
.. ..	... .	. ...	—.—.	—..——	——.—

TELEGRAPHIC FIGURES

1	2	3	4	5	6
.——.	..—..	...—.	....—	———	......
7	8	9	10		
——..	—....	—..—	———		

FIGURE 109

Radio Communication.—"Now," said Jack, "we can hear concerts miles away by radio. The waves used in this form of wireless telegraphy and telephony travel 186,000 miles a second but are longer than light waves. Nature gave us means to detect light waves, but man had to change the energy of the longer waves into a

PHYSICS

form affecting our sense of hearing or of sight. Think of a star as a radio-transmitting set, then our eyes, which see it, are the receiving sets."

Magnetism.—*Jack.* Suppose we stop talking about electricity for a while and learn something about magnets. There is a magnet in every telegraph sounder, in every telephone, and in every dynamo, and I want you to understand how they are used. But we will begin far off and come to these complicated machines by and by. In the first place, Fred, what *is* a magnet?

Fred. A magnet is a piece of iron or steel that attracts other pieces of iron.

Tom. Try your straight magnet on these iron filings, Fred.

Jack. There is a special thing to notice. A bar magnet attracts iron filings, tacks, and so forth, at its ends, but not at its middle. It is just the same with a horseshoe magnet. Try it.

We have learned one thing. Magnets of all shapes attract

FIGURE 110

A straight magnet held in the hand will attract little pieces of iron and will make each of them into magnets, so that they will hold up other small pieces.

Figure 111

A straight magnet—a *bar magnet*—attracts iron filings to its ends, but not to its middle part.

iron filings, tacks, needles, and so forth, to their ends, not to their centers. Here are four little piles of sawdust, of copper filings, of sand, and of coal dust. Try to pick them up with your magnets.

Agnes. They do not move; magnets do not attract such things as sand.

Jack. No; magnets attract iron and steel and nothing else. If you take a pile of copper filings and iron filings mixed together, the magnet will pick up the iron filings and leave the copper. Try the experiment and see for yourself.

Tom. So it does. That is a way of sorting iron out of a pile. If some one told me to pick the iron filings out of this pile by hand, it would take all day to do it; but with a magnet I can do it in five minutes.

Figure 112

A horseshoe magnet attracts iron filings to its ends; but if you try the curved part of the magnet on a needle, there is almost no attraction.

Jack. See what the magnet will do through a pane of glass. Lay a needle on a pane of glass held horizontally and put the magnet under the glass. You will see that the needle moves over the glass as you move the magnet around.

Tom. So it does; glass does not stop the attraction.

PHYSICS

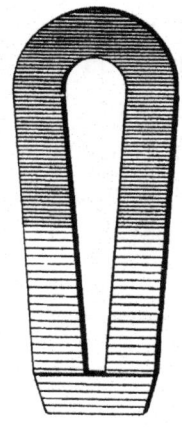

FIGURE 113
A HORSESHOE MAGNET WITH AN IRON BAR (AN ARMATURE) ACROSS ITS ENDS.

Jack. Try putting the needle on a sheet of writing paper or on a piece of silk.

Tom. It is just the same; the needle moves when I move the magnet.

Jack. So much is clear; a magnet is made of iron; it attracts iron and nothing else; it attracts it through silk, or paper, or glass—through anything.

These magnets that you have been using are manufactured. They were made. Let us make some more. Agnes, have you got any needles?

Agnes. Here are some.

Jack laid the needles on the table and rubbed them with the horseshoe magnet, as if he were stroking them with it.[1] He tried each

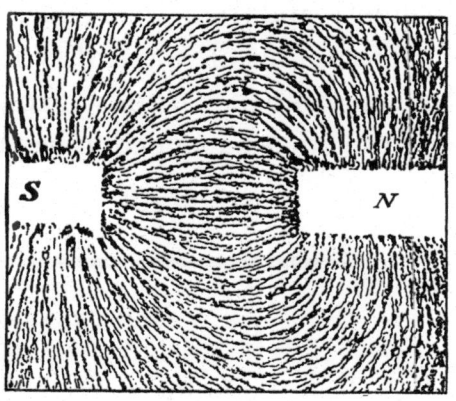

FIGURE 114

Iron filings on a horizontal pane of glass will move into a certain set of curves when you hold a horseshoe magnet underneath the glass. (You must tap the glass gently with your finger tip.)

[1] Make *all* the strokes on *all* needles in one direction, so as to have the needle magnets all alike. Stroke all of them from eye to point, or from point to eye.

139

needle on the pile of iron filings, and every one was able to lift up some filings just as the horseshoe magnet did. Then he took two of the needles and tied a bit of silk about each, near its middle, and hung the silk from two pencils (see Figure 115), so that he had two little magnets, like pendulums. Next he took the bar magnet—a straight

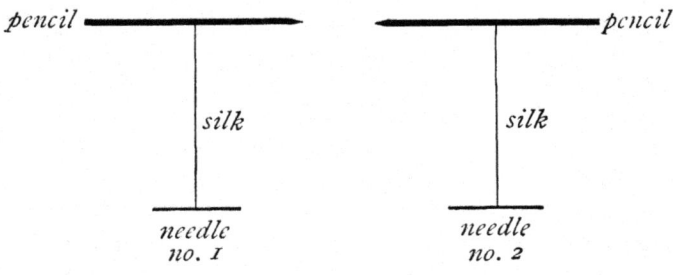
FIGURE 115

magnet—and tried some experiments with needle No. 1 (the other needle was laid aside for the moment). The bar magnet had two ends of course; one was the point, and the other happened to be painted red.

By trials with needle No. 1 he found:

FIGURE 116

1. That the point of the bar magnet attracted the point end of needle No. 1.

2. That the point of the bar magnet repelled the eye end of needle No. 1.

3. That the red end of the bar magnet repelled the point end of needle No. 1.

4. That the red end of the bar magnet attracted the

eye end of needle No. 1.

Then he tried needle No. 2 and found just the same things for it also.

5. The point of the bar magnet attracted the point end of needle No. 2;

6.—and repelled the eye end of No. 2.

7. The red end of the bar magnet repelled the point end of No. 2;

8.—and attracted the eye end of No. 2.

The next thing was to put aside the bar magnet and to try the two needles together. He found:

9. That the two points of the needles repelled each other.

10. That their two eye ends repelled each other.

11. and 12. That the point end of either needle attracted the eye end of the other.[1]

Tom. What is the explanation of all these experiments, Jack?

Jack. It is like this: just suppose there were two kinds of magnetism in the bar magnet. We might call them *point-end* magnetism and *red-end* magnetism, for want of better names. Now when we made magnets out of these needles we put the two kinds of magnetism into them. We put one kind into the point ends of both needles and another kind into their eye ends. Suppose

---

[1] These experiments take some space to describe, but they are so interesting that they should be tried in the schoolroom.

we say that point-end magnetism, wherever it is found, will repel point-end magnetism; and that red-end magnetism, wherever found, will repel red-end magnetism; and that point-end magnetism will attract red-end magnetism, and *vice versa*, wherever they are found. Would not that explain all that we have seen?

Taking all the twelve cases one by one, the children found that the explanation was right. Magnetism of the *same* name repels; magnetism of *different* name attracts. It is not easy to explain in simple words why this is so; but any child who will pay attention and make these simple experiments can prove it.

Natural Magnets.—"These magnets are artificial; they are manufactured," said Jack; "but there are stones that are magnetic to begin with. They were first found in *Magnesia*, a town of Asia Minor, long ago, and the ancients therefore called them magnets."

Mary. In the *Arabian Nights*, in "Sindbad the Sailor," there is a story of a whole mountain made of magnets, so that when a ship came that way the mountain pulled all its iron nails out, and the ship broke to pieces and sank.

Agnes. That isn't true, is it Jack?

Jack. Certainly not, my dear; it is one of the big stories told by travelers. But don't you recollect how they got past the mountain with their ships?

Mary. They built their ships with wooden pins instead of nails and got safely past, so the story says.

PHYSICS

Electro-Magnets.—*Jack.* There is another kind of magnet that I want you to know about. It is made by a current of electricity from a battery passing through a wire wrapped round a bar of soft iron. (See Figure 117.)

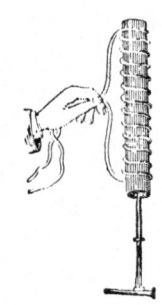

FIGURE 117

You see now how a telegraph operator in New York can make a click on the sounder in Boston. The battery current is flowing all the time except just at the moment when the New York man lifts his key and breaks the circuit.

If wire be wrapped in a spiral around a bar of iron, and if a current of electricity flow through the wire, the bar becomes a magnet and stays so as long as the current is flowing, and no longer.

The electro-magnet of the sounder in Boston is a magnet so long as the current flows, and stops being a magnet the instant the current stops. Whenever the New York man lifts his key

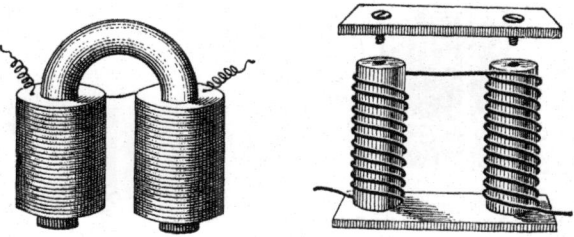

FIGURE 118

Electro-magnets are often made of a core of soft iron bent into the shape of a horseshoe, and wound with wire. The two ends of the wire go to the copper and zinc of a battery. So long as the current flows the iron core is a magnet. When the current stops it is no longer a magnet.

THE SCIENCES

the Boston sounder makes a click—a dot or a dash, just as he chooses. In that way the message is spelled out.

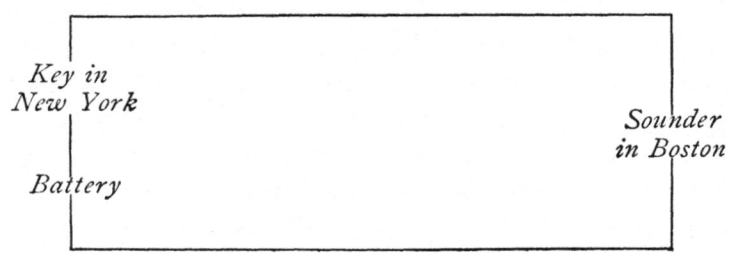

Figure 119

**Figure 120
A Telegraph Key**

Figure 121   A Repeating Sounder

The coils of its magnets are vertical. The armature is fastened to the horizontal bar which moves as the armature moves and clicks against the point of the little screw about it.

**Figure 122
A Cell of
Dry Battery**

Electric Bells.—"Now," said Jack, "it is easy to understand how electric bells work. It is like a telegraph. In the first place you must have a battery. We could make a battery by using several tumblers (like those described on page 133), but it is more satisfactory to buy one cell of "dry" battery, so called.

"We must run our wire along one station to another like this:"

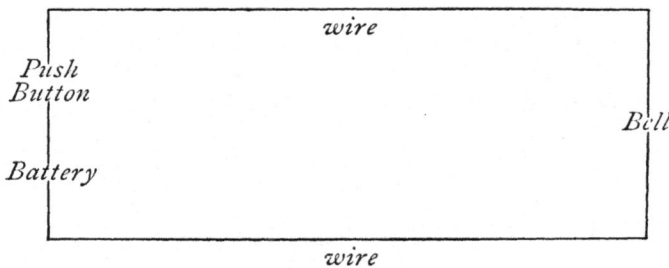

FIGURE 123

The Telephone.—Jack explained the telephone to the children in the following manner. Figure 128 shows the telephone receiver as it would look if it were split down the middle to show what is inside. The coils *H* surround the magnets at *G*. The coils are connected with the line wires, which are inclosed in the casing *F*, and the iron diaphragm *I*, which vibrates so as to copy the voice of the person speaking to you. That person speaks into his transmitter. (See Figure 127.) The vibrations of his voice make vibrations in the diaphragm of his transmitter ; these vibrations are sent along the telephone wire and come to your telephone ; there they make the diaphragm *(I)* of your telephone vibrate just as his voice vibrated;

FIGURE 124 A PUSH BUTTON

It is like a very simple telegraph key. When you push it two ends of the wire are connected so that the current from the battery can flow to the bell and ring it. Until the button is pushed the circuit is broken and the current cannot flow. If you should take away the push button and join the ends of the wire where it now is, the battery current would flow continuously and the bell would ring all the time.

FIGURE 125 AN ELECTRIC BELL

When the push button is touched the current from the battery flows along the wire into the box and round the coils shown in the picture. So long as the current is flowing the soft iron inside the coils is a magnet and attracts the piece of iron which is the hammer (K) of the bell (T). But this piece is a vibrating spring and it keeps moving to and fro and sounding the bell. The moment that the push button is released the current stops flowing and the bell stops sounding.

FIGURE 126
AN ELECTRIC-BELL OUTFIT
COMPLETE

It can be bought in this form with seventy-five feet of wire and staples to fasten the wire.

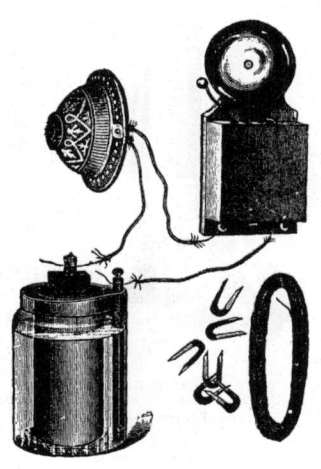

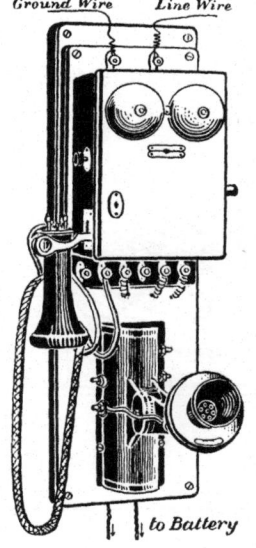

FIGURE 127   THE TELEPHONE

Telephonic conversation can be carried on over great distances as rapidly as if the two persons talking sat in the same room. An electrical impulse passes over the telephone wires from New York to San Francisco in about one fifteenth of a second.

the diaphragm *(I)* makes the air in your telephone vibrate like the speaker's voice, and you hear him speak.

Jack told them about the telephone office and the great switchboards where connections are made between the various telephones. Here busy operators handle hundreds of calls daily. Not only are there local calls, but messages are spoken from long distances. It is remarkable how clearly these messages come. The telephone has brought distant places together.

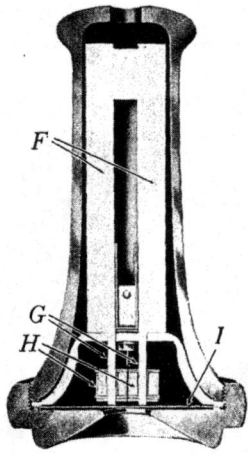

Figure 128
The Telephone Receiver

The Mariner's Compass.—"You know that a magnetized needle points north and south," said Jack. "A compass needle will point to the north no matter to what part of the earth you take it. The reason is that a current of electricity is flowing round and round the earth all the time and that any magnet will always arrange itself at right angles to a current, if it can.

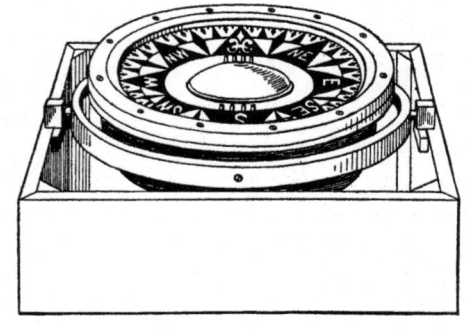

Figure 129
The Mariner's Compass

PHYSICS

The fact is so, and I am going to prove it." So Jack took one of the little magnetized needles (Figure 115) and let it swing freely. It swung so as to point to the north and rested in that direction, thus:

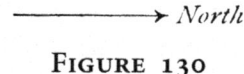

FIGURE 130

Then Jack took the two ends of the wire from his battery and made them parallel to the needle, being careful not to touch the ends together, this way:

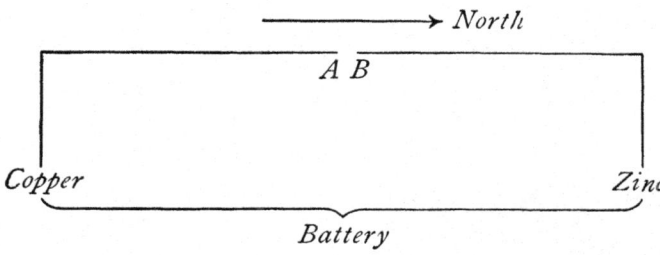

FIGURE 131

No current was flowing, and the needle remained as it was before. Then he joined the ends A and B. A current flowed through the wire, and immediately the needle moved round and pointed west and not north (Figure 132).

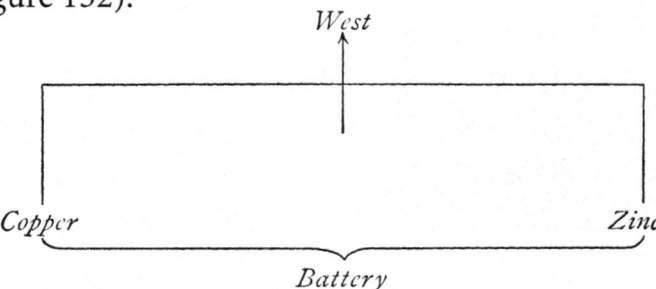

FIGURE 132

THE SCIENCES

"You see," said Jack, "the needle moves so as to be perpendicular to the direction of the current. A current is always flowing round and round the earth from east to west. The sun makes the current. The compass needle is always perpendicular to the direction of the current, and that is why the mariner's compass points to the north. It is a good thing for us that it does so. Sailors can make long voyages and always know which way is north whether the stars are shining or not. They do not need the north star any more."

The Electric Light.—The first electric light was made about a hundred years ago by using a battery of 3000 cells. (See Figure 105.) The wires from the ends of this

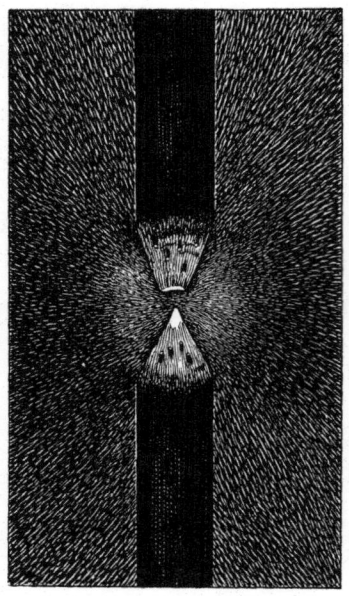

FIGURE 133 THE CARBONS OF AN ELECTRIC STREET LAMP

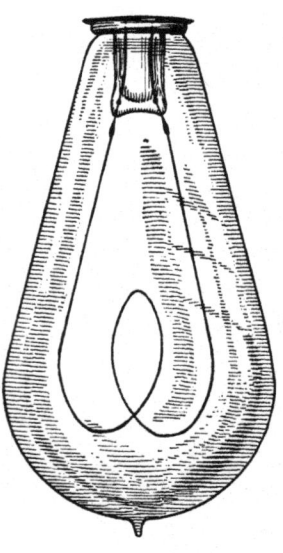

FIGURE 134 CARBON-FILIAMENT LAMP

immense battery were brought close together, and the spark between the ends did not come and go as lightning does, but was steady, like our electric street lamps. The current from so many cells made a great heat as well as a brilliant light. The ends of the wires were melted off where the light was produced, and they were obliged to use *carbon* ends. Today we use tungsten-filament lamps, which last longer and give a whiter light.

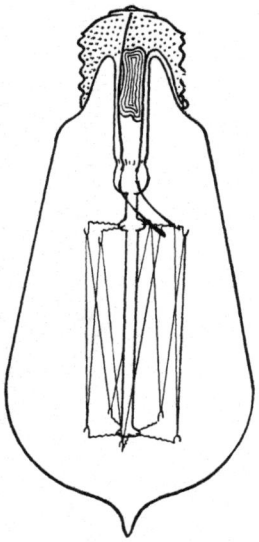

FIGURE 135
TUNGSTEN-FILAMENT LAMP

The Dynamo.—It is possible to make batteries of thousands of cells, like those shown in Figure 105, so powerful as to do the work of electric lighting; but it is very troublesome and expensive. A much simpler and cheaper way to get the current that is needed is to use a dynamo driven by a steam engine.

The steam engine is used to turn a set of little electro-magnets in front of a larger magnet. When this is done a current of electricity flows through two wires leading from the machine, and these wires can be led to the place where we want to use the current—to a distant part of the city to light lamps, or to drive electric cars. Lamps are lighted by letting the current from the dynamo pass through them.

THE SCIENCES

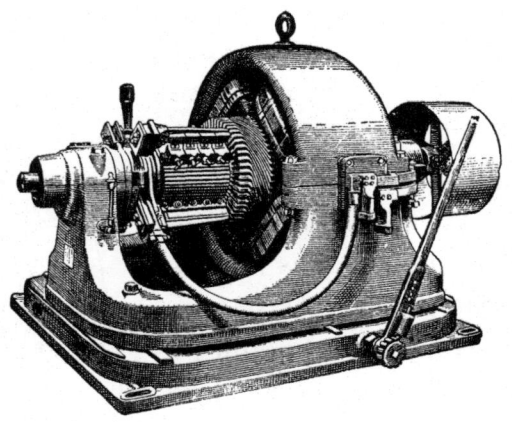

FIGURE 136 A DYNAMO-ELECTRIC MACHINE

A dynamo-electric machine—a belt from a steam engine is put on the wheel at the right of the picture and turns this wheel very rapidly. The central part of the dynamo is a large stationary electro-magnet. Fastened to the revolving wheel (and not visible in the picture) are a number of small electro-magnets. When these small electro-magnets are revolved very rapidly in front of the large magnet a strong current of electricity is made, and this current is carried off on wires to where we wish to use it. It will light lamps or drive a street car, etc.

Electric Railways.—Street cars are driven in this way. Underneath each car is a dynamo (called a *motor*) fastened to the wheels.

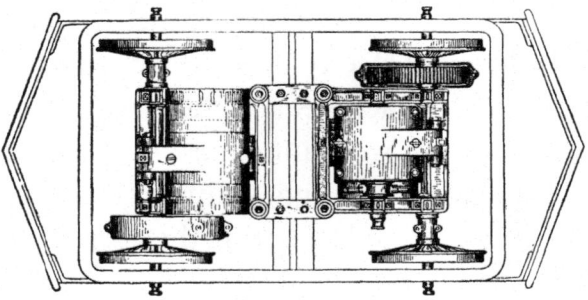

FIGURE 137 PART OF THE FRONT TRUCK OF A STREET CAR (SHOWING THE WHEELS AND THE MOTOR BETWEEN THEM)

PHYSICS

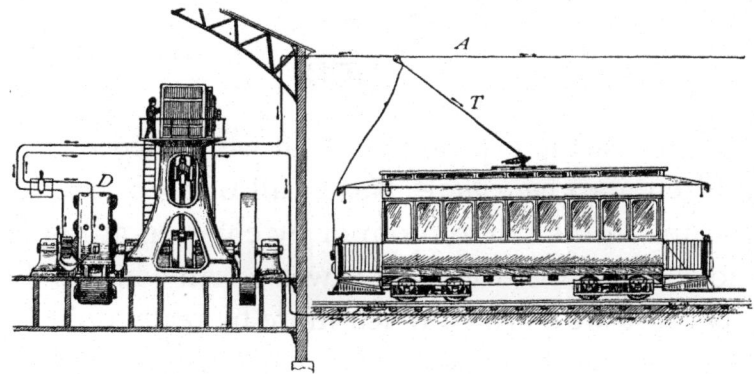

FIGURE 138   AN ELECTRIC STREET RAILWAY

The power house with its dynamo (*D*) driven by a large steam engine is shown on the left-hand side. From this dynamo a current goes out on an overhead wire (*A*). A moving trolley (*T*) on each car takes the current to the motor. The motor turns the wheels whenever the motorman turns the current on, and stops turning them whenever he shuts the current off.

APPENDIX

Some of the experiments that were tried by the children are given here. Nearly all of them can be repeated in the schoolroom or by children at home who will take the trouble. It is well worth while to do it, because we learn so much more by really doing a thing than by merely talking or reading about it. The teacher can readily buy or make the simple apparatus described; and, once made, it will serve for successive classes. Nearly every child has a father, or an older brother, or a friend, who will help him to make these experiments at home if they cannot be seen at school.

What Kind of Things Bodies are.—We need a convenient name for solids, liquids, and gases; let us call them *bodies*, and say that a piece of iron is a solid body, a lake of water is a body of liquid, etc. When we think about any *body* of this sort—a nugget of gold, for instance—we always think of it as filling some space.

Extension.—All bodies are *extended*; they fill a space. Even a sponge fills a space; the holes in the sponge are full of air, and the air in a sponge fills a space and has a shape of its own.

Impenetrability.—Where one body is, another body cannot be at the same time. Putty is soft and can be molded into almost any shape, but where the putty is, nothing else can be at the same time. It completely fills its own space.

PHYSICS

Divisibility.—Every *body* can be divided into two halves, and each of those halves into halves again, and so on. If you will get from the druggist a little piece of *permanganate of potash* (write the name down) and put it into a hogshead of water, you will find that the whole of the water has been colored red. Every drop of water that you take up in your hand is red, and there are millions of drops in the hogshead. That means that the little piece of *permanganate of potash* has been divided into millions of smaller pieces, and that every single drop of water has several of those small pieces in it; for it takes more than one piece to color a whole drop of water.

If you put a piece of *musk* no larger than a green pea (you can buy musk from any druggist) in a room, it will scent the room and everything in it, and it will keep on doing so for years and years. Leave a towel in the room over night, and the next morning every thread of the towel will smell of musk. You could go on leaving towels in the room for a dozen years and taking them away after one night, and every thread of every towel would show that the musk had been near it. That means that every one of the threads of every one of the towels has several particles of musk on it; and it means that the original piece of musk (which seems hardly to grow any smaller) has been divided into millions of little pieces.

Cohesion.—If you take two bars of soap and press them together under a press, you can make one piece out of the two. That piece is held together by a force that we call *cohesion*. All solids are held together by such a force. One part of a lump of iron is held to the other parts by cohesion. It requires a good deal of pulling to pull one part of an iron rail away from the other parts (though it can be done). You can weld two pieces of iron together (by heating) so that they become one piece.

If you stretch a solid body (or compress it) and then take away the force that was stretching (or pressing) it, the body will usually spring back to its first shape. A piece of India rubber stretched (or compressed) flies back to its first shape as soon as you stop forcing it out of shape. A bent steel knitting needle flies back into shape very quickly. India rubber, steel, glass, and indeed most solid bodies, are *elastic*. If you strain them a certain amount, they will spring back into shape like the springs of a buggy. If you strain them too much, they sometimes lose their elasticity like the springs of a farm wagon that has been used to carry very heavy loads. Most solid bodies are elastic; all liquids are so.

Viscosity.—Did you ever see very cold molasses flowing from a spigot? It is *viscous*—a little like a solid and a little like a liquid at the same time. Warm it, and it becomes like a liquid. Tar that is very hot acts like a liquid; as it cools it is viscous; when it is perfectly cold it becomes a solid. Water is not viscous; it flows freely.

All Bodies are Heavy.—All Bodies—solids, liquids, and gases—have weight. A cubic inch of any solid is usually (not always) heavier than a cubic inch of any liquid. Iron will sink in water, but wood will float on it. Iron itself will float on quicksilver. The gases have weight. Air has weight, for instance, as the barometer proves. (See page 89.)

Hardness.—By a little trouble any child can get pieces of soapstone (talc) (1), rock salt (2), fluor spar (4), fieldspar (6), quartz (7). The numbers 1, 2, 4, 6, 7 denote the degree of hardness of these stones. The very hardest stone is a diamond, whose hardness is 10. Rock salt (2) will scratch soapstone (1); feldspar (6) will scratch fluor spar (4); quartz (7) will scratch all of them and will scratch glass, too. You can write your name on glass with a piece of pure quartz. A diamond will scratch *every* stone. If you want to say how hard a stone is, you can give its hardness in a number. Topaz is 8; it will scratch quartz but not diamond.

Ductility.—You can draw some metals out into long fine wires. These are the *ductile* metals, like gold, silver, iron, copper, etc. Glass can be drawn out into fine threads by heating it. Gold can be hammered out into leaves so thin that 30,000 of them, piled one above another, would be only an inch high. If you were to press these leaves under a strong press, they would go back into a gold plate by *cohesion*. (See page 155.) A body is called *malleable* when it can be hammered out into thin sheets. Copper, for instance, is very malleable.

Crystals.—Buy three ounces of alum at the druggist's and pound it into a fine powder and put the powder into a tumbler full of very hot water, stirring the alum in with a glass rod until all is dissolved. Then lay a bit of stick across the mouth of the tumbler with a short string hanging down into the water. (See Figure 139.) Put the tumbler in a cool place and look at it the next

THE SCIENCES

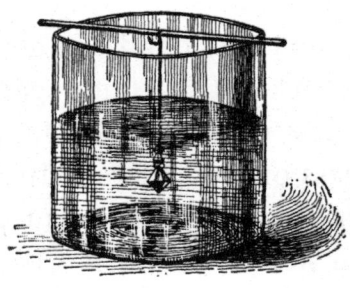

FIGURE 139 HOW TO MAKE ALUM CRYSTALS

day and see the beautiful crystals of alum that have formed. The hot water kept all the alum dissolved. As the water cooled, some alum was freed, and it formed into its own kind of crystal. Everything has its particular way of crystallizing. Alum makes one kind of crystal, quartz another.

You can buy some *rock salt*, some *bichromate of potash*, and some *blue vitriol* at the druggist's also, and make crystals out of these substances, just as you made the alum crystals. Each substance will crystallize in its own way. You can save some of the best crystals in wide-mouthed glass bottles, tightly corked, and begin to collect a cabinet of crystals for yourself.

Freshly fallen snow (that is, frozen water) makes cyrstals, as you can see on a window pane in the winter time.

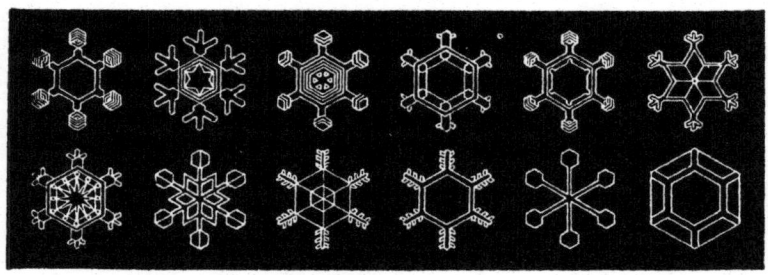

FIGURE 140 DIFFERENT FORMS OF SNOW CRYSTALS

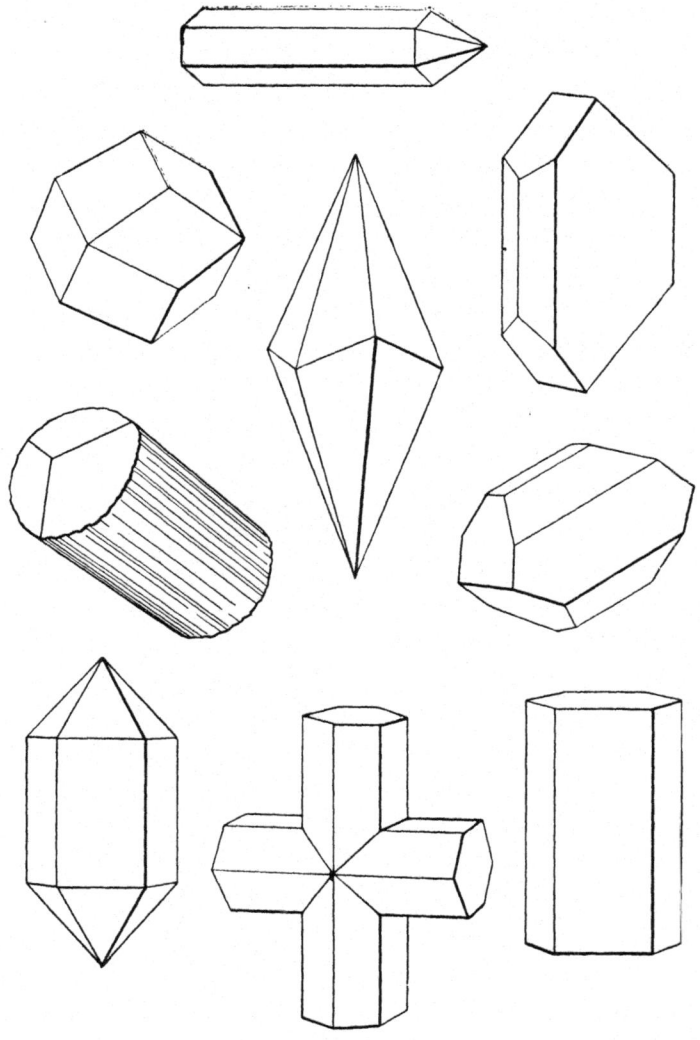

DIFFERENT FORMS OF CRYSTALS

CHEMISTRY

THE SCIENCE THAT TEACHES HOW TO COMBINE TWO SUBSTANCES SO AS TO PRODUCE A THIRD SUBSTANCE DIFFERENT FROM EITHER

NOTE.—*Many chemical experiments can be tried in the schoolroom; but a great number are not safe to try there, and many others require complicated or expensive apparatus. Very many, again, are difficult to explain to children who have had no formal teaching in chemistry. For these reasons the following pages are devoted chiefly to simple and fundamental matters, omitting details, which are instructive only when they are thoroughly understood.*

The children bought at the druggist's small bottles of the chemicals in the list below. Every bottle was labeled with the right name, and they were warned not to get strong acids on their hands or on their clothes.

A glass-stoppered bottle of sulphuric acid
A glass-stoppered bottle of nitric acid
A glass-stoppered bottle of hydrochloric acid
A glass-stoppered bottle of acetic acid (vinegar)
A cork-stoppered bottle with sulfur
A cork-stoppered bottle with iron filings (or tacks)

A cork-stoppered bottle with copper filings (or tacks)
A cork-stoppered bottle with zinc filings
A cork-stoppered bottle with quicklime
A cork-stoppered bottle with chalk crayons
A cork-stoppered bottle with pieces of pure lead
A cork-stoppered bottle with gunpowder
A cork-stoppered bottle with oxide of manganese
A cork-stoppered bottle with sulphur matches

Physical Changes; Solutions.—"Let us take a pinch of this common table salt," said Jack, "and put it in a tumbler of water. What happens?"

Agnes. The water will dissolve the salt. You cannot see it any more. It disappears.

Tom. It is there, though, in the tumbler; for the water tastes salty when I wet my finger with it.

Jack. We can get all the salt back again if we want to, by pouring the salted water on a flat dish and setting the dish on a hot stove. The water will gradually go away, but our salt will be left on the plate. The salt that you put in has not been changed. It is the same salt. It is fit to use on the table, and there is as much of it as there was at first. Now let us try another experiment.

Mixtures.—"Here is some pure sulphur, and here are some iron filings. Take a mortar and bruise the sulphur in it till it is all in fine powder. Now mix the sulphur and the iron and lay the mixture on this pane of glass. Can you boys tell me of any way to separate the iron and the sulphur again, so that you can make one little pile all sulphur and another all iron?"

Fred. Why, I can take a magnet and pull all the iron filings out with it and leave the sulphur.

Tom. That is one way; but it is easier to blow on the pile, and the light grains of sulphur will fly off and leave the heavier iron.

Jack. That is a good way to separate the two things; but Fred's way is the better if you want to save the sulphur. Well, the point is that when you mixed salt and water you could get both of them back again—neither was altered; and when you mixed sulphur and iron you could get both back again—neither was altered.

I want to try a different kind of an experiment. I want to mix two things together and to make a third thing different from either one of them.

Tom. Like mixing a coat and a hat and getting a pair of boots?

Agnes. Oh, Tom, that is silly!

Jack. Well, it is rather funny; and it is not quite so silly as you think, Agnes, though of course it is absurd and impossible the way Tom has said it. No; I want to mix sulphuric acid and iron, one a colorless liquid and the other a blackish solid, and get some green crystals of a substance entirely different from either of them.

Chemical Combinations.—Here Jack took some sulphuric acid in a jar and dropped a few iron carpet tacks in it. In a little while the tacks disappeared; they *combined* with the acid, as people say, and nothing but a colorless liquid was in the tumbler as before. This he poured into a flat china dish which he put on the hot stove. In a little while all the liquid had disappeared and there were left beautiful green crystals; *sulphate of iron*, or *green vitriol*, is the name of them.[1] Then he tried exactly the same experiment, using sulphuric acid and copper carpet tacks, and on the plate there were left beautiful blue crystals; *sulphate of copper*, or *blue vitriol*, is the name of them.

A little finely powdered quicklime combined with sulphuric acid produces *sulphate of calcium*, or *sulphate of lime* (calcium is another name for lime).

"Here," said Jack, "we have combined two things and in each case made a third thing, quite unlike either of them."

> Sulphuric acid + iron = sulphate of iron
> Sulphuric acid + copper = sulphate of copper
> Sulphuric acid + lime = sulphate of lime[2]

---

[1] To make green vitriol take one part, by weight, of iron wire, or tacks, with two parts of strong sulphuric acid in four parts of water and mix. If the mixture is heated, the combination will be more rapid. Filter the resulting fluid, evaporate it over a fire, and obtain the crystals.

[2] To make blue vitriol take one part, by weight, of copper wire, or tacks, with ten parts of strong sulphuric acid (and no water). Mix and boil the acid until gas rapidly escapes. Let it cool and carefully pour off the liquid. Add water to what is left and evaporate it over a fire and obtain the crystals.

To make sulphate of lime take one part, by weight, of finely pulverized quicklime with two parts of strong sulphuric acid and four parts of water. No heat is necessary. When the action ceases evaporate the liquid over a fire and obtain the crystals. The teacher can repeat these experiments in the schoolroom

CHEMISTRY

Chemistry is the name of the science that is busy about such combinations and the changes of one substance into another.

"We have just made sulphate of lime," said Jack, "by combining sulphuric acid and quicklime. Here is another way to get it. This piece of chalk is made out of another acid (a gas) combined with lime.

>Carbonic acid gas + lime = carbonate of lime (chalk)

Chemical Affinity.—"It is as if the carbonic acid were a soldier and the lime a prisoner. Sulphuric acid is a stronger soldier than the other. If I pour diluted sulphuric acid on a piece of chalk, the carbonic acid will fly off in gas and the sulphuric acid will take the lime prisoner in its turn, and we shall have

>Chalk + sulphuric acid = sulphate of lime.

"The carbonic acid has been driven off.

"Vinegar is an acid, too. It is called *acetic* acid. Take some vinegar in the bottom of a tumbler and throw a little lump of chalk into it. What happens? You see the carbonic acid gas flying off in bubbles. It leaves the lime, and the acetic acid takes the lime prisoner.

>Carbonic acid + lime = carbonate of lime (chalk)
>Chalk + acetic acid = acetate of lime

"The carbonic acid has been driven off again.

"Chemists say that sulphuric acid has a stronger

---

after he has himself performed them. Children should *not* undertake them.

affinity for (liking for, fondness for) lime than carbonic acid. It is just as if the prisoner lime *liked* to be a prisoner of one acid better than to be a prisoner of the other. Lead, for instance, likes to combine with nitric acid better than to combine with sulphuric acid, and so with other substances.

"Chemists study these likes and dislikes of the metals, and make use of them. It is much easier and cheaper to get sulphate of lime from carbonate of lime (chalk) by letting sulphuric acid capture the lime than it is to take simple lime and combine it directly with sulphuric acid."

Tom. What is the use of chemistry, Jack? Is it to make new substances cheaply?

Jack. Partly that. The scientific use of it is to explain why two things combine to make a third, and what is the best way to make them do it (for there are many different ways). Its practical use is to teach us how to make such things as gunpowder, glass, soap, vinegar, cheese, leather, gas to burn in our houses, bread to eat, and so forth.

Gunpowder, for instance is a mixture of charcoal, sulphur, and niter.[1] It is a mixture, not a combination, until it is fired off.

Then it suddenly becomes a combination of all three substances, and a great deal of gas is formed. The gas expands in the barrel of the gun, and in expanding drives the bullet out. Chemists have taught us how to

---

[1] Niter is a combination of potassium and nitric acid

make it in the best way. During our Revolutionary War the powder was so poor that men were seldom killed outright as far as a hundred yards. During the World War powder would drive a bullet 800 yards from a machine gun.

Tom. I have seen a book about Benjamin Franklin that says he advised Congress not to arm the soldiers in the Revolutionary War with guns, but with bows and arrows, because they could kill nearly as far off with arrows as with muskets and because they could shoot much faster.

Jack. It sounds absurd nowadays, but it was not at all absurd then. The muskets were better than bows and arrows, even then, but not so very much better. The powder was especially poor. Chemists would laugh at it nowadays.

Mary. What do chemists know about bread, Jack? I think the cook knows more than they do.

Jack. I have no doubt the cook can make bread better if you give her the right kinds of flour and yeast, and so forth; but the chemist tells how to make the right kinds. She uses what he has invented. There are dozens of different kinds of bread for soldiers and sailors and invalids. They were invented by chemists so as to be healthful, or to keep without spoiling on long voyages. The cook could not do that. All the beautiful dyes for silk and wool and cotton (different dyes for each kind of stuff), all the paints, all the inks used for writing and printing, and a thousand things of the sort were invented by chemists. Why, chemists nowadays make indigo—by mixing carbon, hydrogen, nitrogen, and oxygen in the right proportions—that is just as good as the indigo that grows on the plant.

Composition of the Air.—The air of the atmosphere is principally made up of a *mixture* of two invisible gases called *oxygen* and *nitrogen*. Both are invisible and so is the air, the mixture of the two. Water is a *combination* of oxygen and hydrogen. Oxygen gas can be prepared by heating a mineral called *oxide of manganese*. It is made out of manganese combined with oxygen. When the mineral is heated the oxygen goes off as a gas and can by collected in a jar under water. (See Figure 141.)

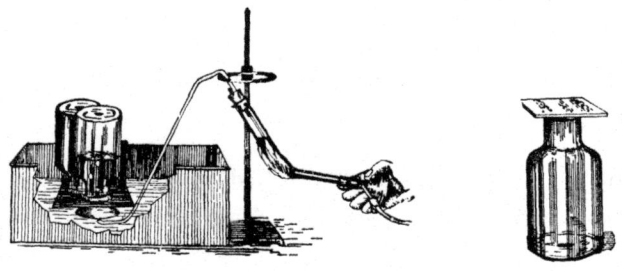

FIGURE 141 PREPARATION OF OXYGEN GAS

Heat powdered oxide of manganese in a test tube one-third full. The oxygen gas will be driven off by the heat and can be collected over water in a jar turned upside down. Afterwards slide a sheet of glass under the jar so as to close it and turn the jar right side up till the gas is wanted for other experiments.

Nitrogen gas can be prepared by burning a bit of phosphorus (not bigger than a green pea) under a glass containing air (air is oxygen and nitrogen mixed). The phosphorus burns up all the oxygen in the air and leaves only nitrogen.

In 100 pounds of air, 23 pounds are oxygen, and

77 pounds are nitrogen. This is the air we breathe. If a live animal (a mouse, for instance) is put into a glass jar that contains nitrogen and no oxygen, it dies. It is not the nitrogen that kills it, but the lack of oxygen. To have life we must breathe; to breathe there must be enough oxygen. Nitrogen helps plants to live, but for men and animals there must be plenty of oxygen.

Combustion.—Combustion is burning. When a match burns there is combustion. All combustion is the combination of something with oxygen. When a match burns, the sulphur on its head unites with the oxygen of the air about it. When a coal fire burns, the coal unites with the oxygen of the air. Combustion is rapid in the case of the match or of the coal, but it is not always so quick. Sometimes it is slow. When iron rusts, as we say, the iron of the outside layers combines with the oxygen of the air and makes iron rust.[1] Rusting is a sort of slow fire without flame, and the iron rust that is left is the ashes. By taking great pains we could even measure the heat that is thrown off while the iron is rusting. A similar kind of slow fire, without flame, takes place in our own body. Air is breathed into our lungs and meets the blood there. The oxygen of the air is carried to all parts of the body by the blood, and our fat and food are actually burned (slowly and without flame of course) in the body. That is the way the temperature of the body is kept up to 98 degrees when the air outside may be down to zero.[2]

[1] Silver and gold do not rust, and that is why they are used for watch cases, coins, and tableware—spoons and forks.
[2] The average temperature of the healthy human body is between 98° and 99°.

A very pretty experiment can be tried by lighting a match, blowing it out, and then putting the glowing red end into a jar of oxygen. The match instantly bursts into flame and burns very brightly. Blow out the match and try the experiment again. The match will burst into flame by itself, as it were, so long as there is any oxygen left in the jar. Even the diamond will burn in oxygen, though it cannot be burned in air.

Hydrogen gas can be prepared by putting some water and a few scraps of zinc in a stoppered bottle (see Figure 142) and by adding hydrochloric acid, which is a combination of hydrogen and chlorine.

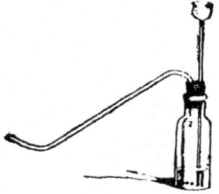 

FIGURE 142 PREPARATION OF HYDROGEN GAS

Put water and scraps of zinc into the stoppered bottle and add hydrochloric acid through the straight funnel. The freed hydrogen gas will escape through the bent tube and can be collected under water and kept for use in a jar. (Leave the jar upside down.)[1]

Hydrogen is one of the lightest of gases. For a long time it was used for the filling of balloons, but it was not suitable for the purpose, as it is highly combustible. Since the World War helium has been used for filling balloons because it is noncombustible and, although twice as heavy as hydrogen, its lifting power is 93 per cent as great.

[1] None of these experiments are to be tried by children.

{Zinc + water} + {hydrogen + chlorine } =

{water + chloride of zinc (these stay in the bottle)}

+ hydrogen (this goes over in the tube)

The hydrogen can be collected as the oxygen was before.

Water.—If hydrogen gas is burned in oxygen (the experiment is not a safe one for the schoolroom), water is produced. Or, again, pure water can be separated by electricity into hydrogen and oxygen. These two gases, both invisible, combine into water—a liquid; and ice—a solid—is nothing but very cold water. That is, solid ice is made out of two gases.

Chemical Elements.—When a chemist sees a substance new to him—a mineral, for instance—the first thing he tries to find out is whether it is a combination of substances that he knows already. For example, he finds that salt is made out of chlorine (a gas) and sodium (a very light metal). Then he tries to see if he can separate chlorine into any other two substances; he cannot do it, or, at any rate, chemists have not done it so far. Neither have they separated sodium into any simpler things. Substances that cannot be separated into simpler substances are called *elements*. Here is a list of the most familiar.

There are twenty-two elements named in this table. If all known elements were included, there would be about ninety names.

Metals	Non-Metals
Aluminum	*Arsenic
Calcium	Carbon
Copper	Chlorine (a gas)
Gold	Hydrogen (a gas)
Iron	*Iodine
Lead	Nitrogen (a gas)
Sodium	Oxygen (a gas)
Potassium	*Phosphorus
Quicksilver (a liquid metal)	Sulphur
*Nickel	
Silver	
Tin	
Zinc	

Every single thing on earth that you can name is made up of one, or two, or three, or more of these ninety *elements*; and it is exceedingly interesting to remember that, so far as we know, everything on the sun, the moon, and the planets is made up in the same way.

Some of the stars and some of the nebulæ may have elements unknown to our chemists, but the solar system—the sun, the earth, and the planets—seem to be all of a piece. Ninety-nine hundredths of all the matter in the solar system is made up of the eighteen elements whose names are not marked with an asterisk (*) in the table just preceding.

CHEMISTRY

Chemical Compounds.—Nearly all the substances that we handle are compounds, not elements.

Diamond is pure carbon.

The black lead of a lead pencil is nearly pure carbon.

Sugar is carbon, hydrogen, and oxygen.

Human hair is carbon, hydrogen, oxygen, nitrogen, and sulphur.

Indigo is carbon, hydrogen, oxygen, and nitrogen.

Quinine is carbon, hydrogen, nitrogen, oxygen, and sulphur.

Air is a mixture of oxygen and nitrogen.

Water is oxygen and hydrogen.

Steel is iron, with some nickel, phosphorus, etc.

Wood is chiefly carbon, oxygen, hydrogen, and nitrogen.

Leather is chiefly carbon, oxygen, hydrogen, and nitrogen.

Human flesh is chiefly carbon, hydrogen, and oxygen, with some sulphur, nitrogen, phosphorus, calcium, sodium, potassium, and magnesium.

Fat is carbon, hydrogen, and oxygen.

Lean is carbon, hydrogen, oxygen, nitrogen, and sulphur.

Milk is water (oxygen and hydrogen), containing fat, etc. (carbon, hydrogen, oxygen, nitrogen, and sulphur).

FIGURE 143 DIFFERENT FORMS OF CLOUDS
a, cirrus; b, cumulus; c, stratus; d, nimbus (rain cloud).

METEOROLOGY

THE SCIENCE OF THE WEATHER

The Atmosphere; the Colors of Sunset.—"I wonder why it is," said Agnes, "that sunsets and sunrises are red. It is the same sun at noon and at sunset, and the same sky; but sunsets are red, and the sky is never red at noon."

Jack. There are two main reasons, Agnes. In the first place, we are looking at the sun through an air that is full of dust; and in the second place, the more dust you look through the redder a thing looks that is beyond. At sunset (and sunrise) you see the sun through a greater thickness of air than you do at noon.

Mary. I do not understand how that is.

Jack. Tom, see if you can explain it by a little drawing.

Tom. Isn't it like this? When the sun is nearly overhead at noon we see it through a less thickness of air than when it is setting (or rising). (See Figure 144.)

Jack. That is right. The greater the thickness of air the more dust there is in it; and, moreover, the more

THE SCIENCES

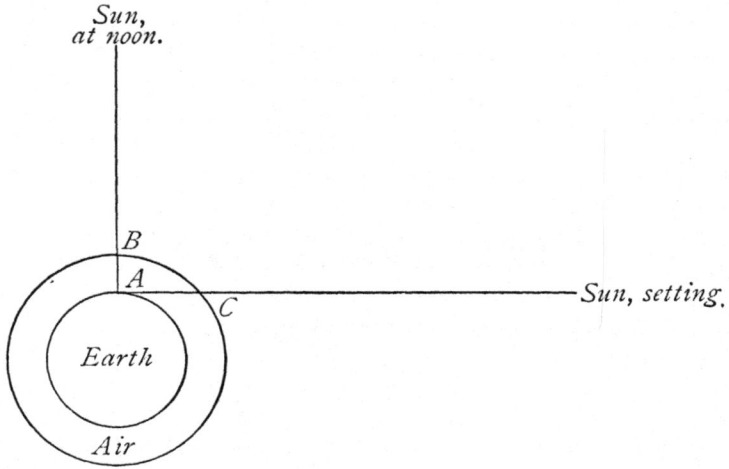

FIGURE 144

A person on the earth's surface at *A* sees the sun overhead at noon through a thickness of air *(AB)*, and the sun at sunset through a thickness of air *(AC)*. AC is considerably greater than AB.

dust the redder the sun looks.

Agnes. How do you know that, Jack?

Jack. Well, you could try the experiment by pointing a long wooden box filled with dusty air at the sun, and then by taking a box twice as long and doing the same thing. But the simplest proof is this: In 1883 there was a huge volcanic eruption of a mountain in Java, called Krakatoa. The whole air for hundreds of miles round was darkened with the dust from the volcano. The winds scattered this dust round the whole earth, so that for two years afterwards all the sunsets in Europe and America were very red indeed, much redder than usual. There was an extra amount of dust in the air at that time, and so the sunsets and sunrises were redder than usual.

METEOROLOGY

It is the same thing in sand storms on deserts. The sun looks red through them.

Fred. Suppose you should go up on a high mountain, what then?

Jack. The higher up you go the less dust you look through. If you are on Mount Washington in the White Mountains (5000 feet high), or on Mount Hamilton in California (4000 feet), the sky looks very pure and blue, and if you go to the top of the high Alps or on Pikes Peak (14,000 feet), the sky is a dark violet color—it begins to look a little black even.

Fred. And in balloons?

Jack. It is blacker yet. The less dust you are looking through the whiter, or the bluer rather, the sun looks to you. If you were quite outside the earth's atmosphere—on the moon, for instance—the sun would not look yellow at all; it would be bluish.

Mary. Where does the dust come from, Jack?

Jack. Oh, from dusty plains, from smoke, the pollen of plants, and from volcanoes. Just think of the millions of tons of coal that are burned every winter.

Mary. Well, then, why doesn't the air become thick with smoke by and by and stay so?

Jack. See if you can answer that, Tom.

Tom. Is it because every rain storm carries the dust particles down with the raindrops? I have noticed that the air is clearer after rain.

Jack. Yes, that is a good reason; and a great part of the dust falls on the ocean, too, and is lost in that way.

Twilight.—"If you will look out any evening half an hour after sunset, you will see a faint arch in the sky in the west that is a little brighter than the rest. That is the twilight arch, and it is caused by the sun's rays reflected and scattered from dust high up in our air. You had better look for it on the next clear evening. It is easy to see.

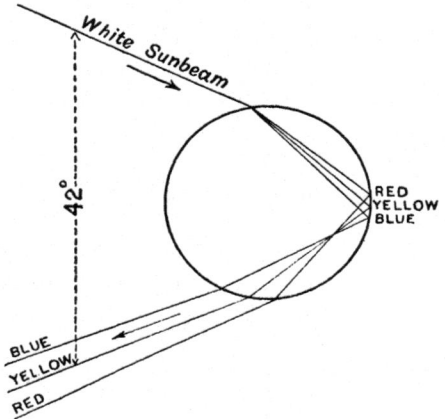

FIGURE 145 WHITE LIGHT ENTERING A RAINDROP IS SPLIT UP INTO COLORED LIGHTS

A white sunbeam enters a hollow raindrop, and its different colors are separated by the water of the drop as they would be by a prism of glass. The white color is separated into red, yellow, blue, and so forth, and is refracted by the drop down to the ground where you are standing. (See Figure 146.) You see the drops by these refracted colors—red, yellow, blue—and all of these colors show in the rainbow.

Dust in the Atmosphere.—"One of the things that physicians want to know is how pure the air is at any place—how free from dust. They put little plates of glass covered with a kind of jelly out of doors and then count the pieces of dust on the glass with a microscope. High mountains and the snowy arctic regions have the purest air of course; but even there there is a great deal more than you would think."

The Rainbow.—"Is the rainbow caused by dust, Jack?" said Agnes; "part of it is red."

Jack. No, Agnes; that is different. You see *all* the colors are in the rainbow, not red alone.

The white light from the sun is split up into colors

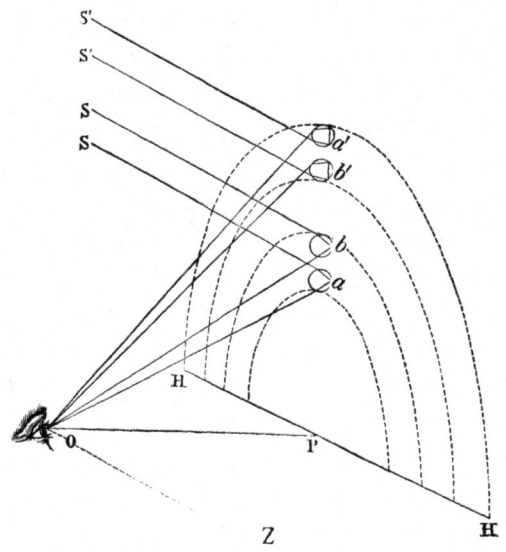

FIGURE 146 THE RAINBOW

Sometimes two bows are seen. Both are formed in much the same way. The ordinary bow is formed by sunlight that enters the top of the raindrops and is refracted to the eye. The secondary bow is formed by sunlight that enters the bottom of the raindrops. (Examine the picture carefully.) S S S' S' are rays from the sun; H H' is the horizon. The center of the bow is always exactly opposite to the sun from where you stand.

by each raindrop much as it would be by a glass prism, and then the light is scattered by the different drops as light is scattered from mother-of-pearl shells. It is not very easy to explain in simple words, but that is the main cause.

FIGURE 147 A COMPLETE SOLAR HALO
(*parhelion*, sundog)

Sometimes the complete halo is seen as in the picture, but more often only parts of it. These halos are caused by light refracted from small prisms of ice in our atmosphere.

Halos.—"You have seen rainbows round the moon, haven't you? and halos—bright circles—round the moon? They are caused by little prisms of ice floating high up in the atmosphere, which scatter the moonlight in a regular way."

METEOROLOGY

Fog and Clouds.—"The air is full of dust that we can see," said Jack, "and it is full of the vapor of water that we cannot see, too. When I put a pan of water out of doors, Agnes, what becomes of the water?"

Agnes. It disappears somehow, if there is not much of it. I don't know where it goes.

Tom. It evaporates; it rises up into the air like a gas. I suppose it is a gas.

Jack. Yes, it is a gas, like invisible steam. Real steam is invisible, and water vapor is invisible. When the water vapor in the air turns into visible water what do you see?

Agnes. Fogs and clouds and mist.

Mary. Yes, and rain and dew.

Jack. Mist and fog are made of millions and millions of little drops of water.

Agnes. Why don't they fall down in rain, then, Jack? Water is heavy.

Jack. The drops are hollow, and they are very small and they float in the air just as soap bubbles do.

Dew.—"When you breathe on a cold windowpane the invisible water vapor in your breath," said Jack, "condenses on the pane and makes a mist which is just like the dew that falls at night. Take a tumbler of ice water and set it in a warm room and you will see dew form on the outside of the tumbler. The cold tumbler condenses the invisible water vapor just as the cold water of a pond condenses the vapor of the air above it into a fog or mist. The reason is because a cubic foot of warm air can hold more water vapor than a cubic foot of cold air. When you cool air, no matter how you do it, you squeeze some of its water vapor out of it."

Tom. When the sun rises the fogs over ponds vanish. Is that because all the air gets warmer and can hold more vapor?

Jack. Exactly so, and when all the air is warm you have no clouds either. Clouds are a sure sign that the air where they are is colder than the other air in the neighborhood.

Agnes. How high are the clouds, Jack?

Jack. Oh, they are at very different heights. Why, don't you know, Agnes, that you are sometimes in the very midst of a rain cloud? The *cirrus clouds* (see Figure 143) are sometimes ten miles high, but usually less. They are probably made of little ice crystals, for the air at that height is very cold indeed.

The *cumulus clouds* are a mile high, or so. The *stratus clouds* are the lowest.

Tom. If clouds are made of hollow water drops like soap bubbles floating in the air, how is it that we ever have rain? Why don't the bubbles always float?

Jack. You have seen two soap bubbles come together and burst? They become nothing but two heavy drops of water, or even one drop, and the water falls. That is rain.

Rain.—"A little sphere of water that is not hollow is a good deal heavier than the air, and a hollow sphere of water is often lighter than air. There are millions of drops in a cloud, and when they are blown about by winds they come into collision and fall in rain.

Size of Raindrops.—"The next time it rains try to measure the diameter of the raindrops. It is not very easy, but you can find some way to do it. I leave it to you boys to invent a way. The raindrops of a heavy pattering summer shower are large—about a tenth of an inch in diameter. Fine rain is made of drops one twentieth to one fiftieth of an inch in size."

Hail and Snow and Sleet.—"I suppose hail is nothing but frozen rain," said Mary.

Agnes. And snow and sleet, too, for that matter.

Tom. Sleet is nothing but snow that is driven about by the wind. In calm weather you get the little snow crystals; but when the wind blows, a dozen of them are blown into one and they come down in little lumps of ice; sleet, that is.

Jack. Or else the snow falls through a layer of rather warmer air and is partly melted.

The Snow Line.—"The higher up you go," said Jack, the colder is the air, and by and by you come to a height above which there is never rain, only snow. That is the line of perpetual snow. In our Rocky Mountains the snow line is about 13,000 feet or so. Above that height the snow never melts at all, and you have snow mountains. In Alaska the snow line is nearly at the level of the sea. That is one reason why Alaska scenery is so impressive. A low snow line makes fine mountains.

Uses of Snow.—"If no snow fell in the winter time, seeds would have a hard time to grow, as the ground would be frozen stiff; but the snow fall covers it up like a blanket. The ground is not frozen so very deep, and the seeds have a chance.

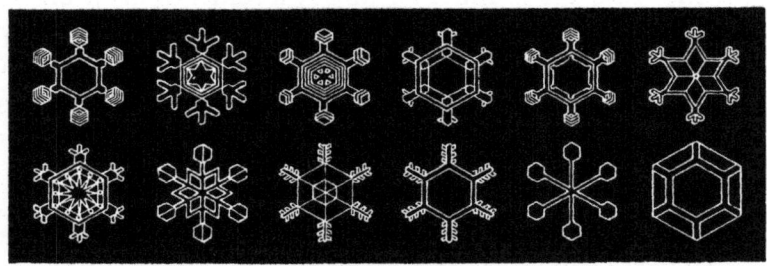

FIGURE 148 SNOW CRYSTALS
Notice that all snow crystals are six sided.

Irrigation.—"Snow has another great use. When it melts in the spring the water can be used for irrigating arid lands. We in the United States let our snow go mostly to waste. We ought to save it in great reservoirs in the western and southwestern states and let it out during the summer when it is sadly needed. Nevada and Arizona and other states could be made into gardens if people would take a little trouble."

Tom. That is something for the government to do. The government must build the reservoirs, and the people will do the rest.

METEOROLOGY

Frost.—"I suppose frost is nothing but frozen dew," said Mary.

Jack. It is not quite that, Mary, though it looks so. The dew does not fall first as water and then freeze; but it really is water vapor frozen in the air, and it falls in fine spikelets of ice and covers everything.

Rainfall.—"How much rain falls in a year, Jack?" said Fred.

Jack. Fred, that is like asking how long the nose of a man is. Why, in some parts of the world almost no rain falls—on the deserts of Sahara and of Arizona, for instance. The average rainfall of the whole world is about thirty-three inches in each year; the water would be about a yard deep at the end of a year if all of it were saved—if it did not get into the soil. But there is an enormous difference in rainfall at different places. On the arid plains of Arizona there are often less than two inches a year. In some parts of the Himalaya Mountains forty *feet* of rain fall in a year.

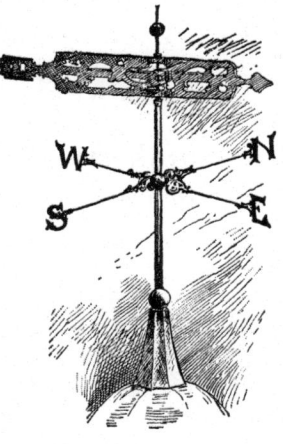

FIGURE 149 ONE FORM OF WIND VANE

The arrow points to the direction from which the wind is coming. If you should move the arrow so as to point in any other direction and then let go of it, you can see that the pressure of the wind on the tail of the vane would soon bring it back. A wind vane put into a rapid stream of water (a brook, a river) would always point upstream. The four arms are set, once for all, so as to point north, east, south, west.

THE SCIENCES

Rainfall and Crops.—"Wheat will not grow by itself where the rainfall is less than about eighteen inches a year, unless there are plenty of fogs. In the arid (dry) regions the farmers have to irrigate their crops."

Winds.—"A wind," said Jack, "is a current of air moving near the surface of the earth. How can you tell which way the wind blows?"

Mary. A wind vane will do that. (See Figure 149.)

Force of the Wind.—"Here is a table," said Jack, that scientific men and sailors use to express the velocity of the wind, or else its pressure on a square foot.

Scale	Description	Velocity in Miles per Hour	Pressure in Pounds per Square Foot
0	Calm	0	0
1	Very light breeze	2	$\frac{3}{100}$
2	Gentle breeze	7 or less	$\frac{23}{100}$ or less
3	Fresh breeze	11	$\frac{64}{100}$
4	Strong wind	18 or more	$1\frac{62}{100}$ or more
5	High wind	27	$3\frac{64}{100}$
6	Gale	36	$6\frac{48}{100}$
7	Strong gale	45	10
8	Violent gale	58	17
9	Hurricane	76	29
10	Most violent hurricane	95	45

"You can describe a wind by using this little table. A wind that blows about eighteen miles an hour—one that would carry a feather or a little toy balloon about eighteen miles in sixty minutes—is called *four* (4). (See the first column of the table.) Such a wind presses on every square foot of a house nearly two pounds. Hurricanes travel at the rate of seventy-six miles an hour—faster than express trains—and press on every square foot of houses nearly thirty pounds."

Agnes. And the houses are often blown down, too.

Jack. They aren't built to resist such winds. We very seldom have them in our part of the world, I'm thankful to say.

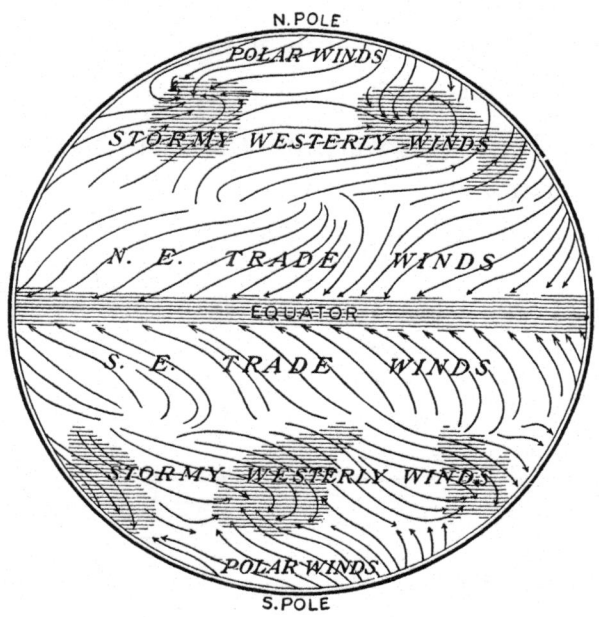

FIGURE 150 A MAP OF THE GENERAL WINDS OF THE EARTH

The arrows show their general direction. The dark spots mark places where there is much rain. These winds blow over large regions of the earth. There are particular winds over smaller regions; but these are, of course, not shown on the map.

Causes of the Winds.—"Whenever the surface of the earth is warm," said Jack, "the air over that part rises and other air from a colder place flows in to take its place. If you boys build a bonfire, the air rises and the smoke rises with it. Other air comes in to take its place, and if your fire was big enough—if a city were burning—it would create a really strong wind. The sun warms the hot regions of the earth, near the equator, more than the arctic regions; the hot air rises and the cold arctic air flows southwards to take its place."

Tom. You have to add that the earth is turning round all the time and so the winds do not flow straight to the equator but in spirals.

Jack. The sun is warming the earth all day—land and water, mountains and valleys; and all night the heat from the warmed places is rising up.

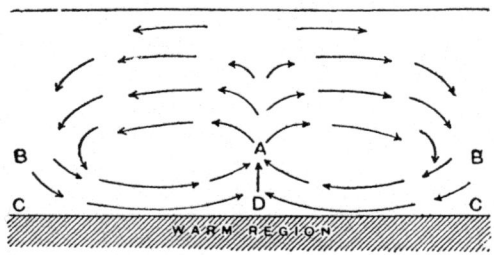

FIGURE 151 DIAGRAM TO SHOW HOW WINDS ARISE

If any region (*D*) is warmer than near-by regions (*C,C*), the air over *D* is warmed and rises. As it rises it cools, and the air near *B,B* moves downwards and inwards to take its place. The air over a bonfire moves in this way, and we have a little local wind. The air over a large part of the Mississippi valley may move in the same way for like reasons, and then we have winds covering several states.

Land and Sea Breezes.—"The land gets warm more quickly than the sea, so that all day the breeze blows from sea to land.

At night the land gets cool sooner than the sea, so that all night the breeze blows from land to sea. The

METEOROLOGY

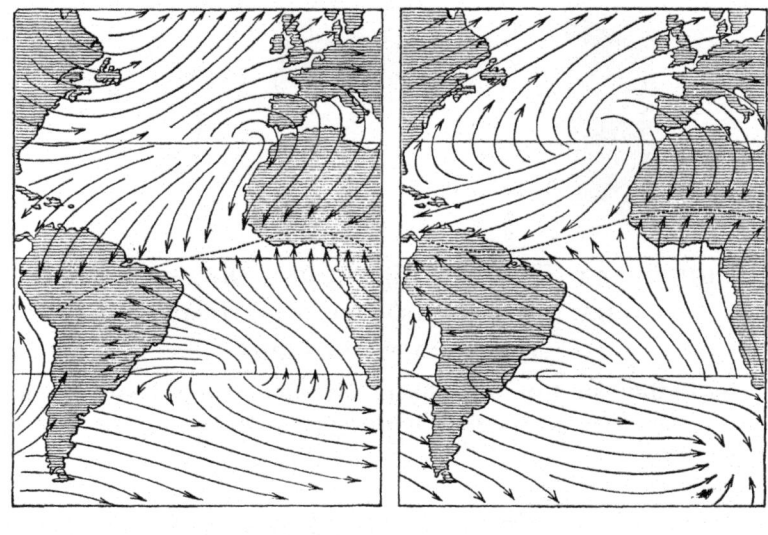

I. In January   II. In July

Figure 152 Winds of the Atlantic Ocean
The arrows show which way the winds blow. Charts like these are made for every ocean and for each month, and sailing ships go by tracks where the winds are favorable.

next time you go to the seashore see if this is not true. Of course there will be other winds, too; but every hot day you will notice the sea breeze that springs up in the morning and blows till nightfall."

Weather.—"Weather depends upon a great many things," said Jack. "See if you children can tell me some of them."

Agnes. Well, we have warm days and cooler nights because the earth turns round. We are in the sun's rays in the daytime and out of them at night. (See Figure 153.)

THE SCIENCES

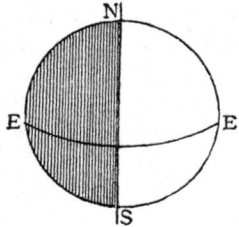 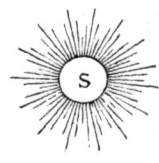

FIGURE 153 THE SUN (S) SHINING ON THE EARTH ILLUMINATING AND HEATING THE HEMISPHERE TURNED TOWARDS HIM

It is daytime in that hemisphere. As the earth revolves on its axis *(NS)* every twenty-four hours both hemispheres are lighted and heated in turn.

Mary. And we have cold winters and warm summers because—I don't believe I quite know why. Is it because the earth is nearer to the sun in summer?

Jack. No, the earth is a little nearer to the sun in December and January than it is in June and July—a little, though not much; there is a different reason, Mary. (See Figure 154.)

Storms.—"Our weather depends on the earth's turning on its axis then," said Jack, "and on its motion round the sun. Those causes are working all the time. Then there are storms that travel over the whole country from west to east[1] and others that come up from the Gulf of Mexico along the Gulf Stream. These storms reach us, and our weather on Thursday, we may say, depends upon the weather some one else had on Monday. The Weather Bureau in Washington gets reports of all the

[1] See Physics, page 92.

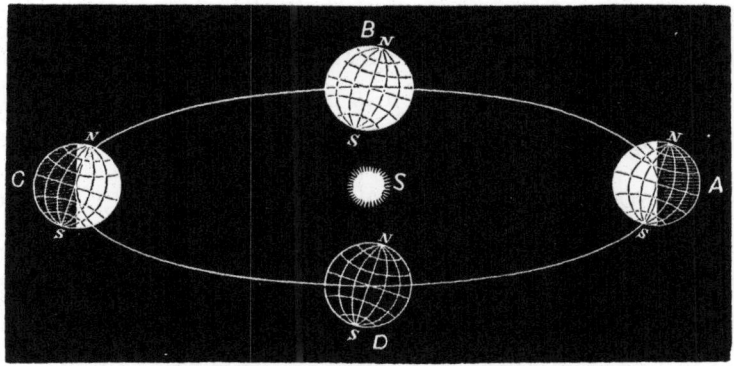

FIGURE 154 THE EARTH IN ITS PATH ROUND THE SUN

The earth is at A in December, at B in March, at C in June, at D in September. NS is the earth's axis, and N is the earth's north pole (in all four positions). At A (December) the arctic regions are dark. As the earth turns round on its axis a person at N is not brought into the light. In the northern hemisphere in March the days are shorter than the nights. As the earth turns a person anywhere in the northern hemisphere is in the lighted half of the earth for a shorter time than in the dark. But in June (C) a person in the northern hemisphere is longer in the light than in the dark—longer in the region heated by the sun.

storms in the whole country by telegraph several times a day and makes up a *prediction* about the weather we are going to have. You see the Weather Bureau predictions in the newspaper every day.[1]

Storm and other Signals.—"Whenever you see a red flag with a black center expect a storm. The triangular pennants tell which way the wind will blow. (See the titles to the cuts.) A square white flag predicts fair weather; a square blue flag predicts rain or snow; a flag half white and half blue predicts local rain or snow storms. A square white flag with a black center indicates

[1] *Ibid.* page 94.

that a cold wave is to arrive. If the black pennant (No. 4) is hoisted above any flag, it means that the weather is going to be warmer. If it is hoisted below any flag, it means that the weather is going to be colder.[1]

"In some regions the Weather Bureau signals are given by steam whistles. A long blast is sounded to attract attention, then follow the signals for weather, and next those for temperature. The signals for weather are long blasts; those for temperature are shorter.

"One long blast means 'expect fair weather.'
Two long blasts mean 'expect rain or snow.'
Three long blasts mean 'expect local rains or snows.'

"One short blast means 'expect lower temperature.'
Two short blasts mean 'expect higher temperature.'
Three short blasts mean 'expect a cold wave.'

"You have no idea how useful these weather predictions are nor how many people read them and follow their indications. Think about it a moment. Suppose there is a cold wave far up in Winnipeg moving eastward. Often it makes cold north winds in Texas—a 'norther'—and northers are destructive to crops and to cattle. The whole of the United States from the Mississippi River eastward to Maine and southward to Florida is going to feel it, and every one is warned to get ready. The railway people are all ready with snowplows;

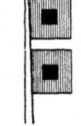

FIGURE 156
HURRICANE SIGNAL

---

[1] These flags are displayed in all towns where there is an observing station of the United States Weather Bureau, and children who live in such towns should learn them by heart.

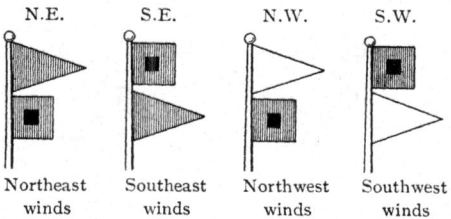

FIGURE 155 UNITED STATES WEATHER BUREAU STORM SIGNALS

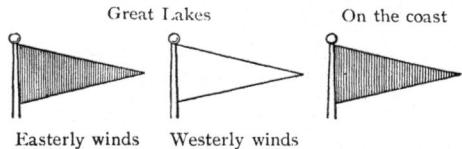

FIGURE 157 INFORMATION SIGNALS

On the Great Lakes a red pennant denotes easterly, a white pennant westerly, winds. A red pennant at seacoast stations indicates a storm.

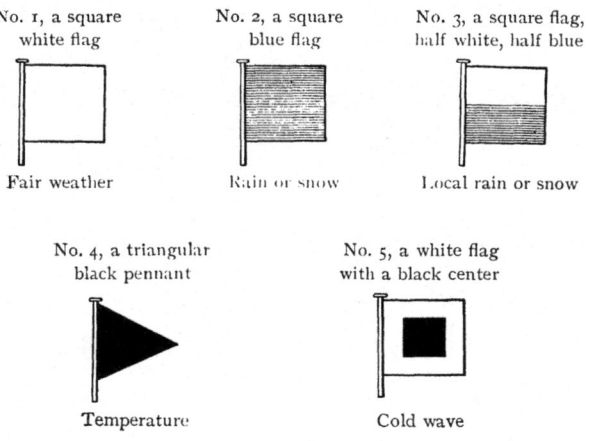

FIGURE 158 WEATHER SIGNALS

By a cold wave is meant a fall of temperature of at least 20° in twenty-four hours. N.B.—In all the foregoing pictures a red flag is marked by vertical lines, a blue flag by horizontal lines.

stock raisers herd their cattle into shelters and provide food for them; people who are shipping fruit, etc., on trains take warning and wait; orange growers in Florida light fires to protect their trees; ice companies prepare to get in their crop of ice; householders see that there is plenty of coal for their furnaces; firemen take extra precautions about their hydrants. There are millions of people who are affected in thousands of ways. The government Weather Bureau warns them all, and every man must look out for himself and for his business. That is the way a government like ours should be, I think. It ought to do the things that no single man can do—like this weather prediction—and leave every man to take care of his own affairs afterwards."

Lightning.—"The clouds in storms are electrified," said Jack, "and lightning is electric sparks on a large scale exchanged between one cloud and another. Thunder is the crackle of the spark echoed among the clouds and mountains. Sheet lightning is usually the reflection of distant forked lightning from the surface of high clouds."

Agnes. Thunder is the echo that we hear, and sheet lightning is a kind of echo that we see.

Tom. How fast does lightning travel, Jack?

Jack. Exactly as fast as light does—at the rate of 186,000 miles in a second—so that the duration of a lightning flash is only a very small fraction of a second. After the flash comes the thunder. Do you know how to tell how far away a thunderstorm is?

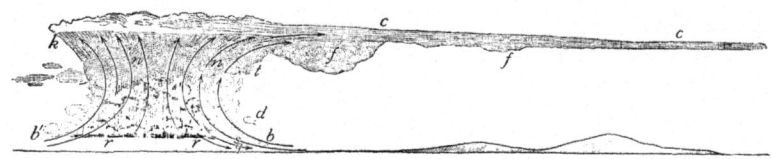

FIGURE 159   SUMMER THUNDERSTORMS

A summer thunderstorm usually occurs in the late afternoon and usually moves from west to east. Several hours before the storm you may see a layer of cirro-stratus cloud *(cc)* high up, with festoons *(ff)* below it. These cirro-stratus clouds may be from ten to fifty miles in advance of the true storm. The air is hot and oppressive—thunderstorm weather. When the cloud *(cc)* covers the sun the air is slightly but noticeably cooler. About an hour later the "thunderheads" *(t)* begin to appear on the western horizon. They are a dull leaden color and threatening. Sometimes distant thunder is heard. The thunderheads rise higher in the air (they are coming nearer), and you can see their bases *(b)* and the gray curtain of rain *(r)* below. The thunderheads are about ten times as high as the curtain of rain. Smaller detached clouds *(d)* are often seen in front of the main storm, which advances eastward. Then comes the "thunder squall" (see the following picture) brushing up the dust in front of it and bringing a rush of cool air. The arrows show which way the winds are blowing in the different parts of the storm. The rain comes in large pelting drops and then in a steady downpour, sometimes with hail, nearly always with thunder and lightning. In half an hour or so the rain is over, the storm has passed, blue sky appears, a rainbow shows in the east, the clouds tower high in the east, and the air is fresh and cool.

THE SCIENCES

FIGURE 160 THUNDER SQUALLS

A part of the preceding picture (within the space marked *d b q* in Figure 159) is drawn on a larger scale here. The first picture shows the thunderstorm as it moves across the country at the rate of twenty to fifty miles an hour. This picture shows the thunder squall as it reaches any particular place. The arrows indicate how the different winds are blowing. If the two pictures are carefully studied, and especially if the reader will compare them with the summer thunderstorms seen at his own home, they will explain most of the appearances he sees.

Distance of a Thunderstorm from the Observer.— *Tom.* You notice the flash of lightning and then count the number of seconds till you hear the thunder; I know that much, but I forget the rest.

Jack. It's like this. The lightning flash and the thunder occur in the storm at exactly the same moment.

You are far off from it. You *see* the flash the moment it occurs because light travels so fast; but as sound travels only 1100 feet in a second, it takes time for the sound of the thunder to reach you. You have to multiply

METEOROLOGY

the number of seconds between the time of the flash and the time of the thunder by 1100, and you'll have the distance of the storm in feet.

The sound of the thunder is heard after the flash by:	The storm is distant:	The sound of the thunder is heard after the flash by:	The storm is distant:
Two seconds.	2200 feet.	Four seconds.	4400 feet.
Three "	3300 "	Five "	5500 " (about a mile).

It takes sounds about five seconds to travel a mile.

Lightning rods.—"Some people say," said Fred, "that lightning rods aren't of any use. How is it, Jack?"

Jack. Well, no lightning rods are so good that you can be certain your house will not be struck. The government takes the greatest pains to protect its powder magazines, but once in a while they are struck. Still, a lightning rod really does protect. It should be a good-sized copper rod that goes deep down into the ground—far enough to reach moist earth—and it should extend ten or twelve feet above the roof, and end

FIGURE 161
LIGHTNING FLASHES

in a sharp point. Three or four good rods will protect an ordinary house almost always. It is better to have them; you are safer.

FIGURE 162   THE GRAND CAÑON
OF THE COLORADO RIVER

PHYSIOGRAPHY

THE SCIENCE OF THE LAND AND OF THE SEA

The Oceans.—The children were looking at a large globe and talking about it. First they turned it so as to show the water hemisphere, then so as to show the land hemisphere, and then so as to show the two poles—arctic and antarctic. (See the pictures, Figures 6 and 7.)

Mary. I never quite understood before how much sea there was and how very little land.

Tom. The books say that three quarters of the surface of the earth are water, and this globe makes you believe it.

"You'd believe it, if you ever made a long voyage by sea," said Tom's father. "Once I sailed straight west for a whole month in the Pacific, from Peru to Tahiti, and at the end of the month I was only halfway across to Australia. I knew all about maps and globes, but I never realized how large the Pacific was until that time. I've had a respect for the mere size of it ever since."

Tom. The Atlantic is large, too, but we don't think of it as so very large because the steamers to England are so very swift. They cross from New York to Liverpool in six days.

THE SCIENCES

Jack. There's another thing. The Atlantic has cables across it in many places and we read the telegrams from Europe in the newspapers every day. That makes England seem near.

**Figure 163
A Deep-Sea Dredge**

It is a large bag or scoop for bringing up parts of the ocean floor. Little shells and so forth are caught by the tassels.

Mary. How deep is the sea, Jack?

Jack. Oh, it is of very different depths in different places. The Atlantic Ocean, on the average, is a little over two miles, and the Pacific is deeper—about three miles. But you know there are places where the sea is much deeper—nearly six miles. Near our new island of Guam in the Pacific there is a spot 31,600 feet deep.

Fred. The highest mountains are about five miles; the sea is as deep as the mountains are high. That is a way to remember.

Jack. Yes; but you must remember too, that there is very much more area of deep sea than of mountain regions, so you could not fill up the sea by putting the mountains in it. You would have to borrow some land from another planet to fill it up.

Depth of the Sea.—"I suppose they find the depth of the sea by sounding with a weight on the end of a rope, don't they?—just as we do in a pond," said Fred.

Tom. They do not use rope; they use piano wire; the rope would float—or at least it would not sink as quickly as wire does.

Jack. Yes, they use miles of fine piano wire and a heavy weight that drops off when it strikes the bottom. That makes it easy to reel the wire in again.

Agnes. What is at the bottom of the sea, Jack?

Jack. Anywhere near the land the sea bottom is covered with mud. The rivers and the rains carry the soil of the land far out to sea and the ocean floor is covered with it.

Little pieces of the rocks of the land are carried out to sea, and you find the same rocks in this mud that we have on the land. The Mississippi or the Amazon river carries its mud out to sea for hundreds of miles. When you get very far from land the dredge brings up a different kind of rock. The little pieces of rock in the sea bottom very far from land have sharp angles. They have not been rolled about by surf and their corners are sharp like crystals.

FIGURE 164

A bit of ocean floor from a region within a few hundred miles of the land. Notice that the fragments of rock are rounded, which shows that they have been washed by waves.

FIGURE 165

A bit of the red clay of the floor of the deep ocean far from shore. Notice that the fragments of the rock have sharp angles, which proves that they have not been rolled about by surf and do not come from the washings of the continents.

Besides these rocks the dredge brings up the shells of little creatures that live near the surface of the sea. When they die their shells sink to the bottom, and there are millions and millions of them, so that a good part of the ocean floor is covered with a kind of *ooze*—they call it—mostly made of these shells. Then we find the bones of fishes, the teeth of sharks, and things of that kind imbedded in the clay; and small pieces of ivory, too, with pieces of meteors which have fallen into the sea. You see the ocean floor is made up of at least three different things—the washings of the continents, the red clay, and the ooze of shells and the like.

Tom. Then, of course, the ocean is full of fish.

Figure 166
A Floating Jellyfish

Jack. There are plenty of fish near the surface. They live where their food is, and most of it is near the surface. There are some fish in the greatest depths, too, but the living things there are mostly crabs, starfish, shellfish, and so forth. You know the surface of the water is crowded with jellyfish of all kinds.

The jellyfish are phosphorescent. They glow when they are disturbed just as a sulphur match glows when you rub it with your fingers in the dark. All the light at the bottom of the sea comes from jellyfish. The sunlight does not go very deep down.

Tom. How do you know there is any light at the bottom of the sea, then?

Jack. Because the deep-sea fish have eyes. If there were no light whatever, all the fish would, in time, lose their eyes, just as the fish in the Mammoth Cave have; but many of the deep-sea fish have eyes.

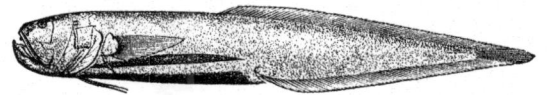

FIGURE 167 A DEEP-SEA FISH WITH EYES

FIGURE 168 A DEEP-SEA SPIRULA,
A KIND OF CUTTLEFISH

The real fish is just twice the size of the picture.

Fred. There are fish—whales and so forth—near the surface of the sea; and there are starfish and crabs and shellfish at the bottom. What is in between?

Jack. Almost nothing, Fred; just dark, quiet, cold water, with no seaweed, no plants, no animals, and no fish. There is no life there to speak of; no light and no motion, for the waves that we see on the surface do not go down very deep either. The middle depths of the ocean are the most dreary and the most monotonous places you can conceive of. The arctic regions are gay compared to them!

FIGURE 169   A FLOATING ICEBERG

Ice is a little lighter than water, and it floats therefore. About one-seventh of an iceberg shows above the surface; six sevenths are below.

FIGURE 170   ICEBERGS BREAKING OFF FROM THE END OF MUIR GLACIER IN ALASKA

Icebergs.—"How do you children suppose an iceberg is formed?" said Jack.

Mary. I suppose the sea water freezes and makes it.

Fred. That will not do, Mary. Don't you see that water could not freeze high up in the air like that?

Jack. Do any of you know?

Tom. Icebergs break off from the ends of glaciers, they say.

Glaciers.—"And glaciers are rivers of ice flowing slowly down from the mountains," said Jack.

Agnes. Do they flow like rivers?

Jack. They flow somewhat as rivers do; yes, only very much slower—a few hundred feet a year, for instance; but they often keep on till they reach the sea (see Figure 170), and there huge pieces break off and form bergs.

FIGURE 171 A BOWLDER OF ROCK THAT WAS ONCE ON THE TOP OF A GLACIER

The glacier brought it from far away, and the rock was left here when the glacier melted.

Tom. Then the water of icebergs is not salt; it is fresh.

Jack. Yes, it is rain water that has fallen as snow, you see.

FIGURE 172 A ROCK ON THE COAST OF MAINE THAT WAS ONCE UNDER A GLACIER AND HAS BEEN WORN SMOOTH BY THE ICE

FIGURE 173 THE BEGINNING OF A GLACIER HIGH UP IN THE MOUNTAINS

The snow of the peaks slides into and down the valleys and becomes ice by the pressure of the tightly packed mass. If you pack a snowball very tight, it becomes nearly pure ice.

Mary. But the sea water does freeze, Jack, doesn't it?

Jack. Certainly; and makes the great ice fields that you have read about.

Some of these fields are very thick, especially when they have been packed together by tides and currents. When the ice first freezes it is smooth, of course, but after it has been packed it is horribly rough. It is often entirely too rough to travel over, and that is the reason why it is so hard to get to the north pole.

FIGURE 174 A SHIP FROZEN IN AN ICE FIELD

Tom. You go as far as you can in your ship, and then you take dog sledges, and finally you come to ice too rough to travel over. Is that it?

Jack. Yes; the ice blocks are as big as houses and are all piled together every which way, and a day's journey is often only three or four miles.

THE SCIENCES

Rivers and Streams.—"Did you children ever think of how a drop of rain water gets from the mountains into the sea?" said Jack. "It is worth while. Suppose you begin by thinking of what happens when the rain falls on a plowed field. The next time there is a rain you must look carefully and see exactly what takes place."

FIGURE 175   LITTLE STREAMLETS OF RAIN WATER RUNNING OFF PLOWED GROUND

Underground Water.—"Part of the water soaks into the ground, but most of it runs off in little streams," said Tom.

Jack. What becomes of the water that soaks into the ground, Agnes?

Agnes. Why, a good deal of it stays there. If you dig down, the ground is always moist.

Jack. And when corn is planted in the field it gets a good part of its water from the earth. You know there is a great deal of water in Indian corn—in the ears and in the stalks; so some of last month's rain will be in the sweet corn you will eat next August. Now, what

PHYSIOGRAPHY

becomes of the water that does not get into the ground but runs off?

Fred. Some of it gets into the air as moisture and makes fog and clouds.

Agnes. Yes, and those clouds may bring rain again.

Mary. But not on our field; they will be far away the next time it rains.

Fred. And most of the water runs off in little streams and by and by gets into the brook.

Mary. And the brook carries it off to the river, and the river to another river, and so on, till it gets to the sea.

Jack. Does the water ever flow uphill?

FIGURE 176   A MEANDERING BROOK

Agnes. No, of course not.

Jack. Then it is downhill all the way from our field to the sea. If you followed a drop of water in the brook, it would always be traveling downhill, but it would not go straight.

Fred. I should think not! No rivers are straight.

Jack. A river in Asia Minor, called the Mæander, was so full of bends that it gave a name to that habit of rivers; we call them meandering rivers, and the bends meanders.

Agnes. Can you say that rivers have habits, Jack?

Jack. Why certainly, Agnes; a habit is a custom, that is all. It is a habit of rivers to flow downhill, to be crooked, to carry little particles of sand and soil in their streams, to roll pebbles and stones along their beds, and so on; it is a habit of rivers to work—they are industrious.

Agnes. Oh, Jack—industrious!

Tom. Well, they are. They carry no end of soil and rocks along in their course, and they work day and night, too.

Jack. You might almost think a river was alive if you counted up all the different things it did, and you might almost say a river had a purpose in life, just as a man has.

Take the Colorado River, for instance; its purpose is to get to the sea in the best way possible, and it has industriously cut a way through rocks till its cañon is

PHYSIOGRAPHY

nearly a mile deep. (See the picture on page 198.) Some rivers actually steal.

Agnes. Oh, Jack! What do they steal?

Jack. Well, for one thing, they steal water from other rivers and carry it away themselves. For instance, the Savannah River has stolen a lot of branches from the Chattahoochee. (See Figure 177.) Then rivers are young and middle aged and old, too; torrents first, and then steady-going, and by and by very mild and gentle; and you might say they are angry when they are in flood. The Yellow River in China has drowned a million persons in a year (1887); the Ganges is nearly as bad; and our own Mississippi has terrible floods.

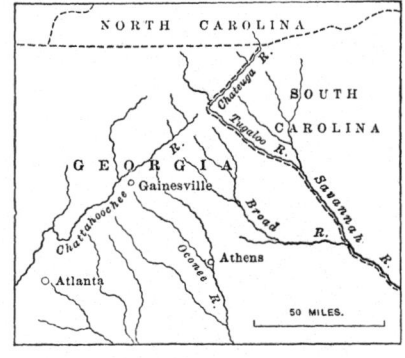

FIGURE 177

The Chattahoochee River formerly owned the waters quite up to the border of North Carolina that now flow in the Chateuga and Tugaloo basins into the Savannah river and so to the sea. It is quite likely that the Oconee river will capture more of the Chatahoochee waters in times to come.

Fred. Anyhow they don't mean any harm, and they *are* industrious; they do the best they know how.

Jack. Industrious they certainly are. In the first place, the water dissolves a great deal of rocky soil (just as water dissolves sugar) and carries it along to a new place. Then a river carries a great deal of sand and mud in its stream and drops that, too, when it can carry it no longer.

Agnes. When does it drop the mud, Jack; when it gets tired?

Jack. You might say so. While the river is flowing fast it can carry a great deal of mud and sand; as soon as it begins to move slower some of this mud falls to the bottom.

FIGURE 178 THE TOWN OF EMS (PRUSSIA) BUILT ON THE NARROW FLOOD PLAIN OF THE LAHN RIVER

Tom. If you want to get dirt out of a wash basin, you have to make the water move quickly. If it moves slowly, the dirt begins to settle.

Jack. They say that the Mississippi carries mud enough every year to make a range of hills a mile long, half a mile wide at the bottom, and five hundred feet high; and the Nile brings huge quantities of soil into lower Egypt. The flood plains of such rivers are the most fertile parts of the world.

FIGURE 179   NIAGARA FALLS
The falls are 165 feet high, and the river is nearly a mile wide just above the falls.

The Land.—"When people talk about the sea," said Jack, "they speak about it as if it were always changing—they call it 'the restless sea'; and when they talk about the land they speak as if the land never changed at all—'the everlasting hills,' they say. Of course it is true that the hills and mountains do not change much in your lifetime or in mine, and of course it's true that if you are at the seashore the waves are never still for a moment; but really and truly the land changes more than the sea does, if you take the whole history of it. The surface of the land is changing all the time."

Mary. I don't quite see how, Jack. I have been here all summer. What changes have there been?

THE SCIENCES

Jack. You have seen the brook to-day. What color was the water, Mary?

Mary. Why, it was clear.

Jack. And yesterday, when it was raining so hard, what color was it?

Mary. It was muddy. Yes, I see; the rain from the ground carried off some of the soil to the brook. It was not much, though.

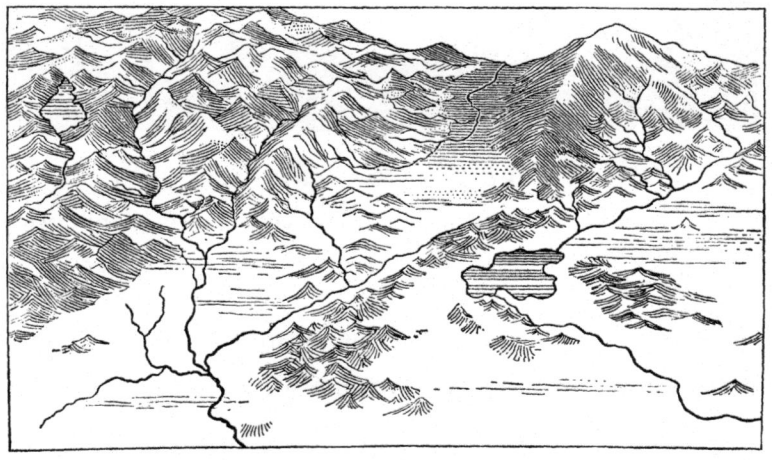

FIGURE 180 A MOUNTAIN RANGE IN CALIFORNIA

The summits are covered with snow which, melting, forms the brooks and rivers; rains model the ravines. Every feature of this landscape has been formed by running water.

Jack. No, not much. But suppose you have a hundred showers every year; in a hundred years there will be ten thousand showers, and every shower will do some work and will carry away some soil. In a hundred centuries there will be a million showers; every one of them will do some work, and all of them together will do a great deal. They will sculpture mountains and level continents.

Mountains.—"Nearly all the mountains of the globe are modeled by water. Wherever there is frost, too, great pieces of rock break off and fall. The shapes of mountains in arid countries like Arizona are modeled by the winds; and then, you know, there are volcanoes, and they change their shape, too. Everywhere the form of the land is changing."

Tom. If all this went on long enough, the earth would be flat.

Agnes. You might say more than that, Tom. You might say that the rains would make all the mountains flat, and that the rivers would carry everything to the sea. Why doesn't that happen, Jack? Why isn't all the land carried into the ocean? Why isn't the whole world flat?

FIGURE 181 SAND MOUNTAINS (DUNES) IN THE RAINLESS DESERT OF THE SAHARA

They are modeled by the wind. Along many seacoasts such dunes are to be found.

Jack. If you gave it time enough, it would be, Agnes; but it would take a great deal of time! The books say that the surface of a whole continent might be lowered an inch or so in a century. North America is, on the average, about 2000 feet (that is 24,000 inches) above the ocean, so you see that it would take at least 24,000 centuries to level it—at least 2,400,000 years. But long before that time other things would happen to prevent. Some of the continents are slowly rising out of the sea all the time, and it is the elevation of whole countries that makes up for the washing away of the land.

FIGURE 182 A CLIFF OF HARD ROCK

The sloping bank at its foot is made up of rock that has fallen from the cliff.

Tom. I never heard of that before, and I don't understand it. What countries are rising now, for instance?

Jack. Well—Sweden is rising, slowly rising, two or three feet in a century. And the northern coast of California is rising, and many other coasts and regions, too. They say the coasts of Alaska and of Peru have been raised more than a thousand feet.

Agnes. Aren't some regions sinking?

Jack. Yes, of course. If one region rises, others will sink. They say the coasts of Massachusetts and of New Jersey are now sinking about two feet in a hundred years; and there are plenty of other places, too, but I don't remember them now.

PHYSIOGRAPHY

Agnes. But, Jack, how can people possibly know that a country is sinking, if it moves as slowly as that? Two feet in a hundred years—why, how can they tell?

Jack. Well, it is not easy, but there are ways to do it. If the sinking keeps on long enough, it is not hard to observe it. For instance, there is a part of the German Ocean not far from the mouth of the Thames where the whole coast has sunk. They say you can even see the remains of buildings at the bottom of the sea when the water is clear. Those were English cities, and the land has sunk within a few hundred years. We know the history of it, I believe. There is a very good way to tell, though, what land has risen out of the ocean.

Tom. What way, Jack?

Jack. By seashells—fossil seashells—found on land, even on mountain tops. Suppose you should find, not one, but thousands and thousands of seashells on the very top of a hill; suppose that the whole rock should be made of them. Well, wouldn't that prove that that particular hill had once been under the sea?

FIGURE 18 FOSSIL SHELLS IMBEDDED IN LIMESTONE

Tom. Yes, you could prove it that way.

Jack. Now suppose that all the hills for hundreds of

miles around were made of shells—of shells of animals that we know cannot live on land, but absolutely must live in salt water—would not that prove that the region had been under salt water long ago?

Tom. Yes, of course. Are there many regions like that?

Jack. Hundreds of them. And in some of them every bit of the rock is filled with seashells. You know what sandstone is, of course?

Tom. Yes, there is a lot of it here. Some of our hills are all sandstone.

Jack. Well, sandstone is nothing but little grains of sand cemented together to make rock; and many sandstones have been formed under water—under salt water. A large river, let us say, brings sand from the shore, and drops the sand grains on the sea bottom. In time the grains are cemented together, and then you have layers of sandstone. By and by something like a

FIGURE 184 THE UPLAND OF NEW ENGLAND WITH
MOUNT MONADNOCK IN THE DISTANCE

PHYSIOGRAPHY

FIGURE 185 A MOUNTAIN IN UTAH FILLED WITH RAVINES, EVERY ONE OF WHICH HAS BEEN MODELED BY RUNNING WATER

great slow earthquake happens, and the sandstone is lifted above the sea. It may be lifted, in time, very high. Then you have layers of sandstone on land. The rains come and wear it into ravines, and parts of it crack and fall, and some of it is covered with soil by the washings of other rivers, and by and by trees and grass grow there, and you have a country like the one we live in.

The earth is not solid down to its center, you know. We live on the outside crust of it. That is solid, of course, and it is about a hundred miles thick. Inside of that crust great parts of the globe are red-hot rocks, like melted lava. It is as if the continents and the oceans were resting on an inside globe of melted rock. The heaviest parts are always pressing down, and the crust is always being strained and bent and cracked. Some parts of the earth are sinking very slowly, and other parts are slowly

THE SCIENCES

rising. Wherever the crust moves you have cracks and when the cracks are large you have long valleys and mountain ridges. (See the picture, Figure 188.)

Stratified Rocks.—"Are all mountains made in that way, Jack?" said Tom.

Jack. Not exactly in that way, Tom. You see it is like this: The crust of the earth sometimes breaks one way, and you have mountains like those in the picture (Figure 188); and sometimes it does not break at all, but bends; it may be pressed or crumpled so slowly that it can yield without much breaking. There is a way to prove this. Do you know what stratified rock is?

FIGURE 186

The earth's solid crust is about 100 miles thick; the narrow line in the picture would be more than 100 miles thick if the diameter of the circle were 8000 miles. Within the crust the rocks are very hot—melted. The pressures in the interior are so great that the rocks, though melted, do not flow like a liquid, but are almost rigid, like a solid.

Tom. It is rock layers—in strata.

Jack. Yes. Now we know that those layers were, in the first place, horizontal. They were layers of sand on the bottom of the sea, or perhaps they were layers of limestone with fossil shells scattered through them. In the pictures (Figures 182 and 189) they have been lifted up so as to keep the layers level; but there are places, many places, where the layers have been crumpled like this:

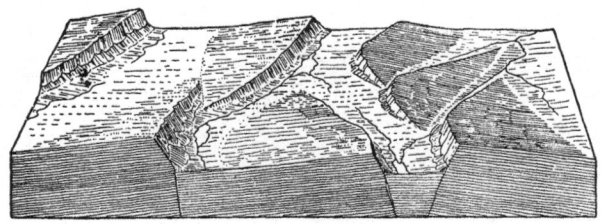

FIGURE 187 MODEL TO SHOW HOW MOUNTAINS ARE MADE BY THE CRACKING OF THE EARTH'S CRUST

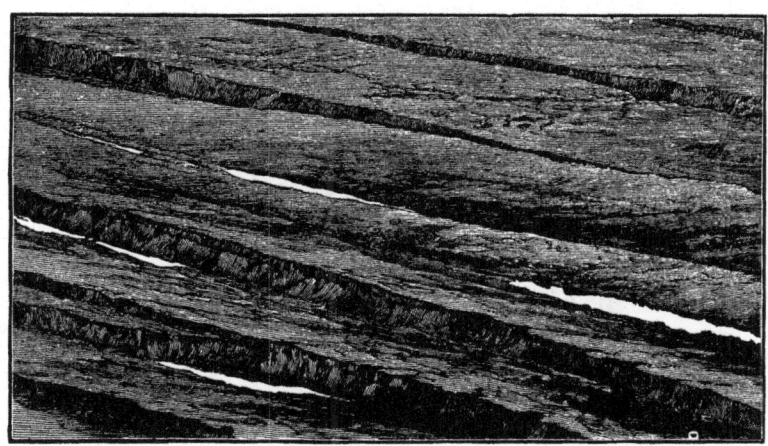

FIGURE 188 VIEW OF THE MOUNTAINS FORMED BY THE CRACKING OF THE EARTH'S CRUST (SEE FIGURE 187)

They are in southern Oregon and northern Nevada and California. The long lakes and the streams lie in the direction of the cracks.

FIGURE 189   A COLUMN OF STRATIFIED ROCK

The rock is made up of nearly horizontal layers. The softer rock between the column and the cliff has been worn away by the waves in the course of thousands of years. Figure 182, preceding, shows a cliff of stratified rock—of rock arranged in layers.

The crumpling makes the crust into mountains and valleys, and you must always remember that just as soon as a mountain is lifted up, it begins to be torn down again by the frosts, the rains, the earthquakes. The older the mountain is, the more its first shape has been altered, and you can tell its age in that way. (See Figures 180 and 185.)

The oldest mountains in America are the Laurentian Hills, near the St. Lawrence River, and the Green and Adirondack mountains. The Green Mountains are about forty or fifty million years old, the geologists say.

Fred. What are the youngest mountains, Jack?

Jack. The youngest in America are the Coast Ranges of the Pacific slope. The books say they are about two or three millions years old. Two million years is young for a mountain. The Wasatch Mountains in Utah are middle aged.

The Age of the Earth.—"Do they know how old the earth is?" said Tom.

Jack. It is not known in the way you can say you know how old a tree is after you have counted the number of rings in its sawed-off stump; but it is known

FIGURE 190

Strata once horizontal are sometimes elevated and folded so as to make mountain ranges, as in the picture, which shows such a case in Maryland. The Appalachian ridges in Pennsylvania (and the Jura mountains in Switzerland) were made in this way.

THE SCIENCES

in a way. Take these very stratified rocks, for instance. They were formed under water by sand which settled down on the ocean floor and slowly cemented into rock. A layer a foot thick will be formed in about 10,000 years, the geologists say. Then a layer 100 feet thick might be formed in about a million years, and a layer ten miles thick in about 500,000,000 years. There is good reason to believe that the earth is at least as old as that, and maybe older.[1]

Agnes. Five hundred million years! I shall never be able to realize that! Why, I can't even understand what a million years is.

Jack. You remember how you children made a model of the solar system?[2] It helped you to understand large numbers, didn't it? Well, you can do something of the same sort here. Suppose that the next time you walk to the village you play that every one of your steps counts for a year. When you have taken 125 steps you have gone back 125 years. Try to remember the name of a famous person who was living then in the United States. When you have taken 1900 steps you have gone back to the time of Christ. When you have walked three miles you have gone back to the time when the first pyramids were built. You would have to walk about twenty miles, each step counting for a year, before you got back to the time when human beings first came on the earth;

---

[1] There is no part of the earth where we can see horizontal layers, one upon another, ten miles thick; but there are places where the layers, once horizontal (—-), have been tilted up (////), so that we can now see their ends and be sure that the original layers were at least ten miles in thickness.
[2] See Astronomy, pages 20-25.

and you would have to walk two or three times round the earth before you got back to the time when the first life appeared on the earth, and much farther yet to get to the time when the earth was first formed.

Mary. It is puzzling, but I think I understand it a little better than I did before.

Jack. Well, my dear, suppose you remember what we have said and think about it by and by. Recollect—a step stands for a year; you were born twelve years ago—twelve steps just take you out on to the lawn. Take a step for each year that has passed since the coming of the Pilgrims. Put in a peg to stand for the coming of the Pilgrims. Over eight hundred steps are necessary to take you back to the landing of William the Conqueror in England; put in a peg for him. A mile will take you back to 600 years before Christ; the city of Rome was founded about that time. Two miles farther will represent the time when the pyramids were built in Egypt; and when you have gone about twenty miles—a year to each step—you will get back to the time that men first appeared on the earth. That is far enough for now. The world was a very old world when Man appeared on it; it had a long history before he came. There had been life long before his time, as we know by the fossils,—shells, fishes, and animals; and there was a long time, nobody knows how long, before that when the earth had no life on it at all—no men, no animals, not even a plant.

Age of Different Parts of the Earth.—"I understand how you can tell when the oldest seashells came," said

Tom, "because you would find their fossils in the oldest rocks—in the rocks lowest down; and if you find a fossil rhinoceros higher up in the rocks than a fossil whale, you would say the whale came first. But how about men? Do they find fossil skeletons of men?"

Jack. Sometimes; but more often they find arrowheads that men have chipped out of flint, along with the fossils of animals. For instance, there are caves where arrowheads and lanceheads have been found along with remains of animals, and where it is plain that the caves were filled up by some accident soon after the men had died; those men and those animals lived at the same time. Sometimes they find the bones of the animals split open, so as to get the marrow out, and blackened with fire.

Age of Man on the Earth.—"Well, that would prove that the men used those very animals for food, wouldn't it?" said Fred.

Jack. Yes, and there is a more wonderful thing still. In one of the very old caves they found bones carved with pictures of reindeer. The man first killed the reindeer with his arrows, and dragged him to his cave and cooked him with fire. Then there was plenty of food in the house. The man felt secure and happy; he had leisure to think and to enjoy himself. And this drawing of a reindeer on a bone made by a half-naked savage is the beginning of all the beautiful pictures in the world. The man was, you may say, our ancestor; and the drawing is the ancestor of all the paintings of modern times.

PHYSIOGRAPHY

Tom. Some one ought to put up a monument to that man! He was the first artist—long before Pheidias and the Greeks.

Agnes. How long before, Jack?

Jack. I knew you were going to ask me that, Agnes. I was sure of it! Well, at a guess, 10,000 years or, it may be, 15,000. It is not certain, like the date of the last eclipse, or the time when Rome was founded. It is twenty miles, Agnes—a year to a step—don't you remember?

Agnes. Yes, I remember; but I don't see how you can tell, though.

Tom. Why, Agnes, if a man eats reindeer in order to live, he must be at least as old as the reindeer, mustn't he?

Agnes. Of course.

Tom. And if the fossil reindeer are found in rocks that it took 5000 years at least to make, then the man must have lived at least 5000 years ago. That is the way they find out.

Jack. That is the way they find out,—yes, Tom; but you must remember that just about 5000 years ago, in Egypt, men were building palaces and temples and pyramids, writing letters to each other, keeping accounts, spinning and weaving, painting and making statues. You have to go back at least 100,000 years to find the earliest men. Agnes, there is a place in the West—Idaho or California, I forget which—where they lately found something very like a doll; it might have been an idol, but it looked like a doll. Now this doll was buried in gravel that had

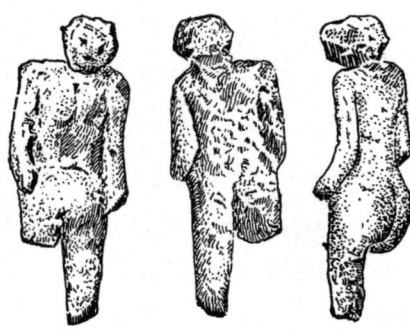

FIGURE 191

been brought down by an old-time river. No one knows exactly how long it took for the river to bring down all the gravel that covered the place where the doll was dropped by the man who had it, but it must have taken thousands of years. Then, long afterwards, the volcanoes near by sent out rivers of lava, and thick sheets of the lava poured out and covered the old gravels and dried up the old river. No one knows exactly how many thousands of years it took for the many sheets of lava to form one above another; but they were more than half a mile thick—that we know. Then came a new river flowing across the lava, and it flowed for so many thousand years that it cut a deep groove for its bed in the hard lava. Scientific men can make a pretty good guess how long each of these different things took. Some men were sinking a deep well in the valley of the new river the other day, and in the well, deep down, they found the doll. You see that we can make a pretty good guess how long ago the doll was made by adding up all the years that were required to deposit the gravel, and to make the lava sheet, and for the river to cut its way in the lava.

Agnes. Yes, I see. I suppose that is certainly the oldest doll in the whole world, though.

The Internal Heat of the Earth.—"You were saying," said Tom, "that the interior of the earth is made of melted rock. I suppose you know that by the melted lava which comes from volcanoes. Lava is melted rock."

Jack. Yes, it is known in that way: volcanoes pour out melted rock. And then geysers send out hot water—boiling water sometimes; and in regions where there are no volcanoes we find that the deep wells always send out hot water—the deeper the well, the hotter the water.

Fred. How deep are the deepest wells, Jack?

Jack. There are some in Europe nearly a mile deep. They are not dug, you know, but are sunk by boring. There are deep wells in America, too; one in St. Louis is 3800 feet deep—more than two thirds of a mile. The water from it has a temperature of 105°. Boiling water is 212°, you know.

Figure 192 A Geyser spouting Boiling Water which comes from deep down in the Earth

Volcanoes.—"You know there are some splendid volcanoes in Hawaii," said Jack; "papa has seen them.

THE SCIENCES

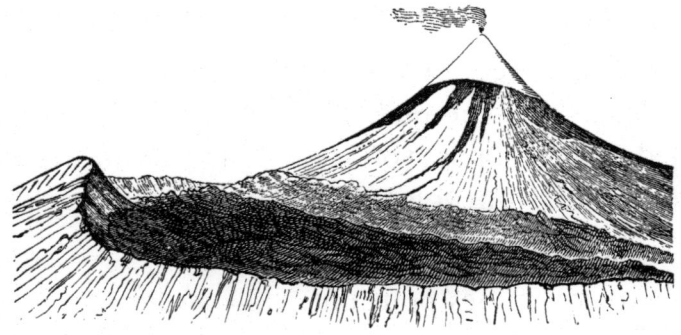

FIGURE 193   THE PEAK OF TENERIFFE IN THE CANARY ISLANDS

The mountain is 12,000 feet high, and its beautiful form has been shaped by the lava streams flowing down from the crater. Notice that the rocks in the foreground form part of a very much larger crater that was active in ancient times and is now extinct.

One of them especially is easy to visit—Kilauea,[1] they call it. It is a great lake filled with red-hot boiling lava that comes up from some reservoir of lava deep in the ground. The lava is liquid rock. Usually it does not flow over the rim of the crater, but sometimes it overflows and sends great streams of red-hot lava all over the country round about and even as far as the sea—fifty miles off.

"Vesuvius, near Naples, is the most famous volcano. You know it buried two whole cities once—Herculaneum and Pompeii."[2]

Agnes. Tell us, Jack.

Jack. Pompeii was a kind of summer resort where

---

[1] Pronounced kē′lou-ā′ä.
[2] Pronounced pom-pā′yē.

the Romans used to go for pleasure. It was a pretty little town full of fine houses, temples, shops, and so forth, not far from the volcano of Vesuvius. Seventy-nine years after Christ (A.D. 79) there was a great eruption, and the ashes began to fall on the city. At first the people were not very much frightened, but pretty soon things got worse and worse, and they began to gather up their movables and to leave the city. A great many of them got away, but hundreds and hundreds were buried in the ashes and died there. The ashes kept on falling for days, and the whole city was covered up. Almost the same thing happened in Martinique in May, 1902. Just imagine what might happen if there were a volcano near New York, and if the city were to be covered up with a thick layer of ashes and not even found again for more than a thousand years!

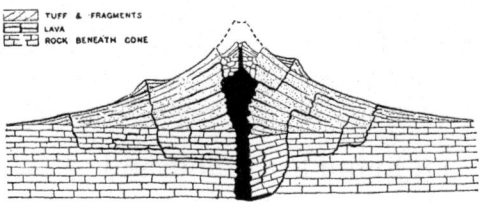

FIGURE 194

A volcano is built up somewhat as in the picture. Underneath it are old rocks in layers. There is a reservoir of lava somewhere underneath them, and a pipe filled with lava leading to the surface. (The lava is colored black in the picture.) When the lava overflows it moves down the side of the mountain like a great river and covers up everything that comes in its way. The upper end of the pipe is the vent, and the lake at the top is the crater. There is often more than one vent. (See the little black lines in the picture leading to different cones.)

THE SCIENCES

FIGURE 195

The picture shows the volcano of Vesuvius as it appears today, and in the foreground a part of the city of Herculaneum after the layer of lava has been taken off. Herculaneum was covered with thick ashy mud and even better preserved than Pompeii, which was buried in showers of ashes. Everything in it was found exactly as it was left—shops, houses, temples, jewelry, tools.

Agnes. Not found for a thousand years!

Jack. Well, Pompeii was buried in A.D. 79, and it was not until 1748 that people began to dig there and found the whole city complete, just as it had been left a good deal more than a thousand years before.

In a baker's shop, for instance, they found loaves of bread all shriveled up, and perfumes and oil and jewelry in other shops. The houses were filled with things that the people used every day; everything was just as before.

Agnes. But the people, Jack—were they found? Were their bodies found?

Jack. Their bodies had mostly wasted away, Agnes; they found their skeletons. One man had come back after his money, and other people after their jewels. The money and jewels were found, and the bones of the persons near them. In one place they found a picture of a watchdog with the sign, *Cave canem*; that means—what does it mean, Tom, in English?

Tom. It means "Beware of the dog!"

Jack. Yes; as we should say "Look out for the dog!" A very great deal of what we know about ancient pictures and statues we learned from Pompeii.

Fred. If New York were buried and dug up a thousand years from now, the people of that time would know how we lived.

Tom. If you went into a house, you would know just what each room had been used for—the kitchen and the dining room and the bedrooms—and just what pictures we had liked and hung on our walls, and what books we read, and everything of that sort.

Mary. And they would know what games we played—tennis and golf; and they might find Agnes' dolls and mine.

Agnes. Just as we found the doll Jack told us about that was buried under the lava in California.

Fred. Are there any volcanoes in the United States?

Jack. There are plenty of mountains that are old worn-out volcanoes, and a few that are still active. Mount Shasta, for instance, in California, is an old volcano, and there are active volcanoes in Alaska, Hawaii, and the Philippines. You children ought to recollect, every time you look at a map, that a very large part of three great states—Washington, Oregon, and Idaho—is nothing but an old lava field. A good part of the lava is 3000, even 4000 feet thick, and it covers thousands and thousands of square miles. All that lava flowed from ancient volcanoes, though it did not flow all at one time; for they find the lava in layers with ashes and soil between, and in some of the soil they find petrified tree trunks.

Tom. That shows the trees had time to grow between one lava flow and the next one, doesn't it?

Jack. Yes, and it gives you an idea how long it took to deposit all that thickness of lava. The doll I told Agnes about was found in this very lava field.

Earthquakes.—"Do earthquakes come from volcanoes?" said Fred.

Jack. There are always earthquakes wherever there are active volcanoes, Fred. You can see that a volcano in eruption which has energy enough to throw huge stones thousands of feet into the air must shake all the ground near it by its explosions. All volcanoes make earthquakes, but very many earthquakes are not caused by volcanoes.

Mary. What does cause them then, Jack?

PHYSIOGRAPHY

Jack. Suppose you lay a book flat on its side, Mary, and imagine that the book is part of a layer of rock that was once deposited at the bottom of the sea. Now take another book and lay it flat on the first one. That stands for a second layer of rock—perhaps a different kind of rock—lying over the first layer. Now you know the crust of the earth is moving slowly all the time, sometimes up, sometimes down. Suppose both those layers of rock were lifted so that one end of them was higher than the other. Tilt the books, Mary, and keep tilting them, and see what happens.

Mary. Why, one book slides off the other.[1]

Jack. That is exactly what sometimes happens to great beds of rock. They lie flat in the first place. Then they are slowly tilted, and by and by one of them slides a little—a very little—on the other. Ten million tons sliding only a little way—an inch perhaps—will make a terrible shock that can be felt for hundreds of miles around. The Charleston earthquake was caused in just that way.

The geologists say that the layers of rock underneath South Carolina lie one on another like the two books, and the earthquake was caused by the sliding of the layers. The rocks I am talking about were deep underground, you know. When they moved, the rest of the rocks moved, too, just as a pile of bricks will slide when you move some of the bottom ones; all of them moved. A good part of Charleston was wrecked, you

---

[1] The simple experiment should be tried in the schoolroom, choosing two books with smooth covers.

THE SCIENCES

FIGURE 196   THE CHURCH OF SAINT AUGUSTINE IN MANILA, PHILIPPINE ISLANDS, AFTER THE EARTHQUAKES OF JULY, 1880

know, and all the eastern part of the United States was shaken more or less. Why, they even felt the shock at Boston, at Toronto in Canada, at Chicago, at St. Louis, and at New Orleans. The shock was not severe there, but it was felt.

Tom. Of course an earthquake is weaker and weaker the farther you go away from the center of it.

Jack. Yes; like the little water waves in a pond when you throw in a stone. That is a "waterquake," you might

PHYSIOGRAPHY

say. You know the waves are larger and higher at the center, and become smaller as they move out. All of South Carolina was badly shaken, so that chimneys fell. The shocks were strong enough to frighten people in Georgia, in Ohio, and in Pennsylvania, and they were felt as far as the Mississippi River, and farther.

Mary. Were many people killed, Jack?

Jack. Only a few, Mary. They ran out of their houses, and lived in the parks for several days till the shocks were over.

FIGURE 197   VIEW OF PART OF CHARLESTON, S.C., WRECKED BY THE EARTHQUAKE OF AUGUST, 1886

THE SCIENCES

Agnes. Oh, did the earthquake last for days?

Jack. There were shocks every now and then for several days, but only a few really severe ones. You see it took several days for all those rocks underground to settle down and be quiet. There was an earthquake in the Mississippi Valley once (1811) that lasted nearly a year. The people camped out of doors for months and months.

Agnes. Might we have an earthquake here, Jack?

Jack. Certainly, we might; no one can tell. There are not many earthquakes in the eastern part of the country, and those that we have are usually light; you need not be afraid of them. If an earthquake comes, go out of doors and keep away from houses—that is all. But there are earthquakes everywhere—light ones. You boys can prove it if you want to.

Fred. How can we prove it?

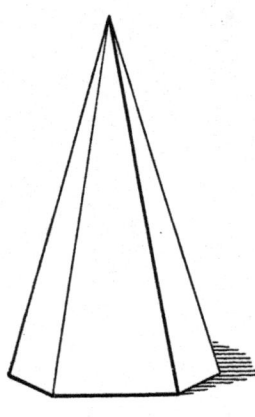

FIGURE 198
PYRAMID

Jack. Get some pieces of nice wood—red cedar, for instance—and make two or three pyramids. (See Figure 198.) Then cut off a little of the top of each one of them, and stand them upside down in a steady place—on the mantelpiece of a room that is not used much, for example. When a slight earthquake comes—one too slight for you to feel perhaps—the house will be shaken and the mantelpiece, too, and the pyramid will fall on one of its sides. Try it.

The boys did try it. They made half a dozen pyramids and cut off a little of the top of each one, and stood them about in different places in the house and in the barn. They often would find one of them fallen on its side, and they usually discovered that the housemaid, in dusting, had caused that particular earthquake. But every few months they found *all* the little pyramids thrown down, and most of them lying in one direction; and then they knew that there had been a light shock—too light for them to feel, but strong enough to overturn their "earthquake detectors," as they called them. The direction in which the detectors lay on their sides showed the direction in which the earthquake wave was moving—north and south, for instance.

The Lisbon Earthquake.—"They say the Lisbon earthquake was one of the very worst," said Tom; "do you know about that, Jack?"

Jack. It was one of the worst, certainly, because there was not only an earthquake, but a great sea wave too. The people ran out of their houses to take refuge in the churches, and then the churches fell and crushed them. Many went to the wharves so as to be away from falling walls, and a huge wave from the sea—eighty feet high, they say—rolled in and drowned thousands of people.

Fred. A wave eighty feet high! What made it, Jack? Was it a part of the earthquake?

Jack. No doubt the level of the sea bottom was

changed somehow, and the water rolled in like a great wall. That often occurs in South American earthquakes. A strange thing happened to one of our war vessels once. It was the *Wateree,* and she was at anchor in the bay of Iquique[1] in Peru (1868). All of a sudden came a great wave from the sea and tossed the ships about like boats, and it carried the *Wateree* far inland and left her there high and dry. Think of it—one of our war ships with all her guns and men (no one was hurt) high and dry on land!

Fred. What did they do? Could they get her off?

Jack. No; and so the government took away all her cannon and everything that was valuable, and sold her to a Spanish gentleman for a summer house!

Agnes. I think that's funny. A man-of-war for a summer house!

Jack. That is not the funniest part of it, Agnes. A few years later there came another great sea wave, and it lifted up the *Wateree* and carried her a long way farther inland, and there she is now, a summer house for a different family.

---

[1] Pronounced ē-kē′kā.

Lightning Source UK Ltd.
Milton Keynes UK
UKOW01f0319160917
309277UK00001B/88/P